Superwave

Super Recipes

Bob and Paul Bowersox

Superwave
Super Recipes

Bob and Paul Bowersox

Food Styling and Photography by Bob Bowersox

SoxMedia LLC

Published by SoxMedia LLC
Robert T. Bowersox, President

Written by Bob and Paul Bowersox
Food Styling and Photography by Bob Bowersox
Bowersox Brothers Photos by Pete Checchia, Philadelphia

First hardcover edition 2010

Please read and adhere to all manufacturer's manuals
before operating any kitchen device.

Printed by Book Printing Revolution, Minneapolis, MN USA

ISBN: 978-1-4507-4330-3

ISBN 978-1-4507-4330-3
90000>
9 781450 743303

Contents

Acknowledgments

First and foremost, we'd like to acknowledge the true gift of love of food and cooking that was imparted to us by our parents, Don and Marilee Bowersox. We know that wherever they are, they're "side by each" in a kitchen, just as they were in nearly 50 years of marriage.

And also to you, the viewers and customers of The Sharper Image and ShopNBC: without you, nothing happens.

Our sincere thanks to Mary and Marla for allowing us the time to disappear into the kitchen and not come out for days (and honest, we cleaned up). And to Cindy Kazarian of Kazarian Spencer Ruskin, Los Angeles: no better agent on the planet.

And thanks to Eddie, Jeffrey, and Steven Mishan, Jack Guindi, and all our friends at Emson. We appreciate the opportunity and the support.

Thanks also to The Sharper Image. We've always loved you guys.

Kudos and a great job to Mark Pitzele at Book Printing Revolution. And to Rachel Sherwood and Impressions Styling – we'll say it again: you're one of the very best.

And finally, thanks to ShopNBC and all our friends there, particularly Rod Ghormley, Keith Stewart, Bob Ayd, Paul Kelley, MaryIda Lira, Sarah Berglund, and Jim Pritchett. You guys ever thought of moving somewhere warmer?

Introduction

Culinary tools, to my brother Paul and me, had always been basic – each had a specific purpose, each had an individual ability and procedure that you used to deliver an expected outcome. You used one thing for this kind of cooking, another for that. It was the way we were raised.

Take our mother's kitchen, for example. I can't tell you how many times one of us would get a dressing down for using her "chicken skillet" – a much-beloved electric fry pan – to cook up some bacon, or her good omelet pan in the oven to broil up a steak. You'd have thought we were trying to do a load of wash using dirt instead of detergent.

I suppose to Mom there was a certain order to this, but it without doubt made for crowded cabinets, given that she had a pan for pretty much every different kind of cooking she did. And, as budding young chefs, we felt a bit limited in the creative aspect. Half the fun of cooking is in the experimentation, isn't it?

Flash forward a few years and you find the two of us working in my restaurant, The Crepe Chalet, and the word "basic" had begun to evolve. Because on the line at the Chalet, it was as basic as it came: give us 8" and 10" skillets, a couple of saucepans, some tongs, a chef's knife, a spatula, a cooktop and an oven, and we could make pretty much anything on the menu.

And now today, the wonder of technology has changed the concept of "basic" for us again. Because The Sharper Image – the leading name in innovative household technology – has given us what we like to call the first true cooking *instrument* ("tool" just doesn't seem to cover what this wonderful piece of equipment is): The SuperWave Oven.

The SuperWave truly is a culinary wonder. It is the culmination of years of slow progress toward consolidation, of developing a single instrument that can handle any kind of cooking. And not only is it a great multi-tasker, but it does a brilliant job with all the types of cooking you ask it to do. It bakes like the finest restaurant convection oven. It broils and sears like a salamander broiler. It barbecues like your outdoor grill. It roasts like your grandmother's old steel gas oven. It fries with air instead of oil, making for healthier, tastier dishes, and it can dehydrate using that same air flow. One instrument does all this and more. Basic at its most evolved.

Our mother would have had a stroke. She never would have believed that one item in her kitchen could have cooked anything she imagined.

But that's just what Paul and I decided to do when The Sharper Image came to us and asked us to write this book for you – Imagine. We knew you'd been asking for more recipes to make in your SuperWave…from basic family fare to the kind of gourmet creations usually found in the finest restaurants.

So that's just what we've given you. We cover all the main categories –

Starters offers great appetizers and finger foods, from authentic Italian Bruschetta to Chipotle Chicken Wings for the big game.

Fowl enhances the original SuperWave cookbook with dishes that go beyond roast chicken – gourmet plates like Game Hens Stuffed with Mushrooms and Wild Rice, and Duck Breasts with Balsamic-Onion Marmalade – and bring it back to the fun of Hawaiian Shish-Kabobs, or Jalapeno Chicken.

In Beef, we take you from the family favorite of Stuffed Peppers and Grandma's Classic Meat Loaf to the haute cuisine of London Broil with a Cabernet Reduction Sauce or Filet Stuffed with Oyster and Proscuitto.

Pork and Lamb offers basics like Pineapple Glazed Ham and several takes on Pork Chops, as well as beautiful renditions of Roast Pork and some of the best Baby Back Ribs you'll ever get your fingers sticky with.

And nothing cooks Seafood like the SuperWave. From Seared Tuna, Seafood Cakes, Mahi-Mahi and Salmon dishes, to restaurant-quality creations like Sole Stuffed with Crabmeat, Thai Crab Imperial, and Lobster Medallions with Shrimp and Scallops, you can't miss with the way the SuperWave does them.

We offer up Sides that will become family favorites, like Garlic Mac and Cheese, Crusty Parmesan Potato Wedges, Roasted Asparagus, and Gingersnap Squash.

Baked Goods brings you neighborhood bakery ideas, from Scones to Hot Pepper Corn Bread, Applesauce Cake to a Never-Fail Cheese Souffle that will have your guests marveling at your culinary abilities.

And what would a cookbook be without Sweet Things, right? How about Chocolate Drop and Butterscotch cookies, Southern Sweet Chocolate Pie, Caramel Bread Pudding, and the always fun Chocolate Whoopie Pies.

We've also included two special chapters that we think the SuperWave does wonders with: Casseroles – from the classic Shepherd's Pie and Tuna Fish Casserole to the marvelous Boatman's Stew and Asian Cashew Chicken Casserole – and Meatless Main Dishes, which includes terrific creations like Garden Lasagne, Vegetarian Pizza (Bob's favorite), Veggie Burgers, and SuperWave Samosas (Paul's favorite).

So enjoy looking through this book. There's not a bad recipe here. And enjoy even more cooking in your Sharper Image SuperWave Oven. We know it will be hard for you to believe that one instrument can deliver all of this and more, but that's exactly what the SuperWave Oven does.

You see, it's the new basic.

SuperWave Oven Tips

The recipes in this book were specifically designed and tested in Sharper Image SuperWave Ovens. In certain cases, there were steps to the recipes that involved stovetops, but for the most part, the SuperWave does the bulk of the cooking.

Please refer to the Instruction Manual that was included with your SuperWave Oven, reading and following all warnings, precautions, and important safeguards included there. While the SuperWave is incredibly easy to use and master, you should still be aware of its limitations and potential hot spots. You'll also find a number of great tips and ideas that the Sharper Image folks have learned will make the SuperWave even more successful for you.

In designing and testing the recipes, we came across a number of additional tips that we think you'll find useful:

- When using casserole dishes, tart dishes, cake pans, etc., choose dishes that are no more than 1-1/2" in depth. Since the SuperWave is a little over 10" in diameter at the base of the bowl, you can use up to 10" pans. And don't fill them all the way to the top – leave about one-eighth to one-quarter of an inch for the ingredients to expand. Unless you're just browning off the top of the dish when it's finished the main cooking, always place the casseroles on the bottom rack.

- And always use the racks for meats. It helps to drain away the fat and not allow its reabsorption.

- If adapting a recipe from another cookbook, keep in mind that you'll have to adjust the time by up to a third. The SuperWave is very efficient. You may also have to adjust quantities to fit the capacity of the Oven.

- Don't use foil in the SuperWave. It blocks the Infrared, and can also be pulled up into the convection fan.

- We've found that thinner is better than thicker when it comes to meats. Choose cuts of beef or pork that are no more than 2-1/2" thick at most. This also applies to rolling meats for roulades, etc. Don't roll them larger than 2-1/2" in diameter, and roll them loosely. And when cooking anything with real depth, use the lower rack.

- When cooking anything with longer cook times, use the lower rack. The halogen is so efficient and hot, you want to keep the foods away from it when cooking for longer periods of time.

- When baking in pans or dishes, always use the lower rack, unless they are very shallow.

- When making Whole Meal Ideas, make sure the food time that will require the most time is on the top rack, where the oven will be hotter. That way you won't overcook what's on the bottom rack, for instance, the vegetables.

- No pre-heating is necessary, if using recipes from another source. The Tri-Cooking Technology is so efficient, the oven is virtually up to temperature immediately.

- When toasting anything, always use the top rack, but keep an eye on the food – the Super-Wave is very quick. When toasting something like bagels or breads, you may want to spin them halfway through the cooking period, to make sure they toast evenly across, and if you want them toasted on both sides, make sure to flip them. And if a recipe calls for nuts as a topping, feel free to use raw nuts, as they will easily toast during the cooking process because the oven is so efficient and the halogen gets to a searing/roasting temperature.

The more you use the SuperWave, the more nuanced you'll find it. As you get used to how it cooks, you'll find that you'll instinctively know where to put certain foods, and what to put them in. It's really very simple, and you'll learn fast, believe us.

A Note On Dehydrating:

Dehydrating fruits, vegetables, and herbs is easy in the SuperWave, but takes some time to do, so never start the process unless you have the time to remain near the oven to keep an eye on the food as it goes through the dehydration process.

Create a grid with the two racks (the short on top of the tall), and spray them lightly with a cooking spray before placing the fruit, vegetables, or herbs on them.

When preparing the fruit or vegetables, you have to slice them fairly thin, about 1/16" to 1/8" thick. For some softer fruits, like bananas, figs, or peaches, it may be a good idea to set them in the freezer for a short time – not until they're frozen, but until they are firmer. They'll be easier to slice thinly then.

Place the slices in one layer across the racks – you may have to do several batches. Set the temperature dial to "Thaw/Wash", which will correspond to about 170°, which is the perfect dehydrating temperature. Set the time for 60 minutes, but keep an eye on things – some fruits and vegetables will give up their liquid faster, which means they'll tend to get over-done. So watch them carefully. Because of the SuperWave's convection air circulation, you should not have to turn the slices.

For certain things, like potato chips, you might want to brush them lightly with vegetable oil, and then sprinkle the slices with salt, barbecue-flavored salt, or other flavorings when you first put them in. Experiment a little…have some fun creating your own flavors!

A Note On Cleaning:
One of the best things about the SuperWave Oven is that it cleans itself! While the bowl is

dishwasher safe, you may want to just fill it with about 1-2" of water and a good squirt of your favorite dishwashing liquid. Turn the Temperature Dial to "Thaw/Wash", and the Time Dial to about 8 minutes. The SuperWave does the rest! After the bowl has cooled, just rinse it in the sink and dry it off before reassembling the oven.

Cleaning the lid can be done with a damp cloth, or a paper towel sprayed with a little window cleaner. Make sure the lid is unplugged and cool before wiping it off inside and out.

Starters

Bruschetta

PREP: 15 minutes   COOK: 6 minutes   MAKES: 12

Bruschetta is one of those savory appetizers that work equally well as a snack for the boys watching Monday Night Football or for a fancy dress cocktail party. It's light, full of complex flavors and never fails to satisfy. Originally meant to be toasted over coals, bruschetta is even better with the Superwave Oven where you get all of the flavor without the time, mess and hassle of charcoal. It has become the go-to hors d'oeuvre at our family gatherings.

2 TBS Water
2 oz Feta, crumbled
1 tsp Green Onion, minced
1 clove Garlic, crushed
½ tsp salt
    Dash Black Pepper, course ground
1 Roma Tomato, chopped fine
¼ cup Red Bell Pepper, minced
1 TBS Parsley
2 TBS butter
12 slices demi Bread, (2-3 inch diameter breads)

Mix all ingredients, except for the bread. Butter bottoms of bread, place on high rack in SuperWave Oven and spoon mixture on the top of each slice.

Bake at 400° for 6 minutes. Serve warm

Variation: In Italy, they keep their Bruschetta simple, and that's perfect for the SuperWave. Here's a recipe we picked up from friends in the medieval Tuscan town of Montisi: First, toast the bread on one side on the top rack until golden brown. Remove from the oven and <u>immediately</u> rub each slice with large garlic cloves cut in half...the garlic should literally melt into the bread. Then wash the toasted, garliced bread with olive oil (don't skimp). Top with chopped tomatoes, then with very thin ribbons of fresh basil leaves (again, don't skimp). Give each a dusting of salt and pepper, and Mangia!

Baked Brie

PREP: 3 minutes   COOK: 8 minutes   SERVES: 4

At the end of a rough day, nothing beats sinking into a deep couch with a glass of fine red wine, your sweetheart at your side and this dish served up with crusty bread and some fresh apple slices. Our parents always insisted that simple pleasures are the best, and this dish proves it. After all, what could be simpler than bread, cheese and fruit? A loaf of bread, a jug of wine, and WOW!

1 small round Brie or 1 slice of Brie Cheese
2 Green Onions, minced
1 tsp Basil, dried and flaked
¼ cup Red Bell Pepper, chopped fine
   Coarsely ground Black Pepper
1 TBS Butter

Tear off a piece of aluminum foil as long as it is wide. Place the brie in the center of the foil and fold the foil up around the brie to create a wall extending slightly above the cheese itself.

Spread the onions, peppers, black pepper and basil evenly over the top of the brie and inside the foil well. Top with the pat of butter.

Bake on the lower rack in the SuperWave Oven for 8 minutes at 350°.

Oysterette Munchies

PREP: 10 minutes   COOK: 10 minutes   MAKES: about 4 cups

We've been asked for this recipe more than any other. It's one of what we call "cousin" recipes: our father received it from a cousin, who received it from HER cousin, who...you get the idea. These wonderful, tiny bites take no effort to make, but they may be the best crunchie-munchie you've ever made for yourself or your family. Watch out, though – once you start nibbling them, it's very difficult to stop.

3/8 cup Vegetable Oil
½ tsp chopped dried Dill
¼ tsp Garlic Salt
½ tsp Lemon Pepper
1 package Hidden Valley Ranch
   Original Salad Dressing Mix (dry)
1 7½ oz. box of Oyster Crackers

In a medium bowl, whisk together the oil, dill, garlic salt, lemon pepper, and dry dressing mix.

Put the crackers in a bowl, and pour the herb mixture over the crackers and mix them well, so that they are coated well with the oil and herbs. Place half the crackers in a round 8" or 10" nonstick cake pan on the bottom rack of the SuperWave.

Bake at 300° for about 5 minutes. Shuffle the crackers with a spatula, so they turn, then bake again for another 5 minutes or until they are crusty and the herbs are dry on them. Remove and cool.

Spinach Balls

PREP: 20 minutes (not including cooling)   COOK: 5-7 minutes   MAKES: about 3 dozen balls

Our mother was born and raised in West Virginia, home of Appalachian wild onions known to the natives as ramps. Their flavor comes in somewhere between shallots and garlic and they grow everywhere in the hills and hollers of "The Mountain State". We found this recipe in Mom's old file, but in the original, she had minced ramps in place of the onions listed here. These balls double nicely as a side dish for any meat main course, as well.

1 10-oz package of frozen, chopped Spinach
1 cup herb-seasoned Stuffing Mix
½ cup Onion, finely chopped
3 Eggs, beaten
¾ cup Butter or Margarine, melted
¼ cup grated Parmesan Cheese
2 tsp Garlic Salt
¼ tsp dried Thyme
2 tsp dried Dill

Cook and drain the spinach, and place in a large bowl. Add the remaining ingredients and mix well. Chill for about 30 minutes.

Roll a handful of the cooled mixture between your palms to form balls just large enough not to fall between the tines of the SuperWave racks.

Place the balls about ½" apart on the tall rack. Bake at 300° for about 5-7 minutes or until cooked through. Serve hot.

Sausage Balls

PREP: 20 minutes   COOK: about 10 minutes   MAKES: 2 dozen balls

Every autumn we attend a party hosted by long-time family friends in the hills of northeastern Pennsylvania. We all join in to make apple butter, and we tap last year's keg of hard cider and toast the harvest . We also make these snacks from the bounty of fresh sausage we have on hand. They are wonderful any time of year, of course, especially when served with sweet mustard, but they are especially good when shared with friends.

1 pound bulk Sausage (hot or mild)
1 pound Sharp Cheddar Cheese
3 cups Bisquick

Mix all the ingredients in a large bowl, preferably by hand. Roll a small handful of the mixture between your palms to form a ball about 1" in diameter (large enough not to fall through the tines of the SuperWave racks).
Place the balls about ½" apart on the lower rack. If you have to split this baking process into two cycles, do so. Bake at 375° for about 10 minutes or until cooked through. Serve hot.

Chipotle Chicken Wings

PREP: 20 minutes   COOK: 15 minutes   SERVES: 4

The smoky heat of chipotle, combined with the garlic sweetness of the sauce take this bar food favorite and put it completely over the top. This may very well be the best chicken wing sauce we have ever tasted. It strikes an entire melody of flavors instead of hitting a single note as do so many others we've tried. One word of warning, though......it's hot enough to get your attention, so keep a cold one on hand in case of emergency.

1 (7 ounce) can Chipotle Peppers in Adobo Sauce
½ cup Water
½ cup White Vinegar
½ tsp Salt
1 stick Butter
1/3 cup Onion, chopped
2 cloves Garlic, minced
1/3 cup Roma Tomato, chopped
1 bottle Louisiana Hot Sauce
Juice of ½ Lemon
1 tsp Honey
¼ cup Catsup
1 pound Chicken Wings
Garlic Powder (for wings)

Place the chipotle peppers in a blender and add the water, vinegar and salt. Blend on high for 1 minute.

Melt butter in a saucepan and add the onion, garlic, tomato and the bottle of Louisiana Hot Sauce. Stir well and let the mixture cook for about five minutes, stirring occasionally. Pour into blender with the chipotle pepper sauce. Blend on high until smooth. Add the lemon juice, honey and catsup, and blend again for a few seconds. Pour back into the saucepan, and let it simmer and thicken for 10 minutes.

Rub the wings with the garlic powder and brush liberally with the sauce.

Place wings on the tall rack of the Superwave Oven and bake at 350° for 15 minutes. Serve with bowl of sauce for dipping or brushing on the wings.

Chicken Liver Pate

PREP: 15 minutes   COOK: 17 minutes   MAKES: 2 cups pate

Dad was a preacher's kid who grew up in the rural outskirts surrounding York, Pennsylvania. Being a relatively poor parish at the time, Hickson Bowersox, our grandfather, was often paid in chickens, dairy goods and vegetables donated by the farm families who attended his church. His wife, Charlotte, made the best of all they got, and used just about everything but the cluck of those chickens. This is one of her recipes we've updated with the addition of brandy and spices.

1 stick Butter
1 Onion, chopped
1 pound Chicken Livers
4 TBS Brandy
1 tsp Dry Mustard
½ tsp Nutmeg
¼ tsp Cloves, ground
½ tsp Black Pepper, coarsely ground
  Pinch of Cayenne Pepper
  Salt to taste

Melt the butter and place in an oven safe d with onions and chicken livers. Broil on th top rack in the SuperWave at 400° for 7 minutes.

Puree the onion/liver mix in a blender or food processor. To this, add brandy, mustard, and spice Blend well. Refrigerate. Serve on bread rounds or crackers.

Black Bean Quesadillas

PREP: 8 minutes   COOK: 6 minutes   MAKES: 4 quesadillas

Growing up in Colorado introduced us to delicious Mexican food long before Tex-Mex became a widely recognized cuisine. Our sister Maggie and her husband Ken, who still live just outside of Denver, have taken that early exposure and turned it into an art form of delicious proportions. This is one of their triumphs that we think you will make over and over again. The key to the recipe is the fresh cilantro and basil which round out the flavor and send it soaring!

1 (15 ounce) can Black Beans, drained and rinsed
¼ cup Roma Tomato, chopped
3 TBS fresh Cilantro Leaves, chopped
¼ cup Black Olives, chopped
8 (6-inch) Flour Tortillas
4 ounces Pepper Jack Cheese, grated
¼ cup fresh Basil, chopped
½ cup Salsa of your choice

In a food processor, process the beans, tomato, cilantro and olives until smooth.
Place the tortillas on a work surface and spread the bean mixture evenly onto the tortillas. Sprinkle with the cheese, basil and salsa. Top this with another tortilla.

Place a tortilla at a time on the tall rack of the Superwave and bake at 400° for 6 minutes, turning once, until cheese melts. Cut into wedges and serve hot with sour cream, if desired.

Spiced Nuts

PREP TIME: 10 minutes   COOK TIME: 15 minutes   MAKES: 4 cups

These sweet, spicy, slightly salty nuts make a great snack and are absolutely de rigueur for a Fall party. They also make great toppings for desserts or salads. Take them along for a healthy pick-me-up during a stroll, hike or bike ride. We favor almonds or pecans if you want to use only a single type of nut, although the deluxe nut mix at your local market makes for a fun and delicious selection to savor.

¾ cup Sugar
¾ tsp Salt
1 tsp Ground Cinnamon
½ tsp ground Cloves
¼ tsp Allspice
¼ tsp ground Nutmeg
1 Egg White, slightly beaten
2 ½ TBS Water
3-4 cups Nuts (almonds, cashews, peanuts or a mix)

Mix the sugar and spices. Gently add in the egg white and the water, blending thoroughly with a whisk or fork.
Add the nuts, a half cup at a time. Stir with a fork until well-coated. Lift out with forks and place on a lightly-greased or nonstick 8" round cake pan. Place pan on the low rack of the SuperWave.

Bake at 275º for about 15 minutes. Remove from the oven and cool for 15 minutes. These can be stored in a covered container.

Variation: If you'd like to sweeten these instead of spicing them up, substitute a tablespoon of brown sugar for the cloves, allspice, and nutmeg. Follow the directions as written.

Fowl

Game Hens
Stuffed with Mushrooms and Wild Rice

PREP: 30 minutes   COOK: 30 minutes   SERVES: 4

Cornish game hens were bred so that all of the meat in the bird is white meat and each bird is a single serving. Stuff those little darlings with a succulent blend of wild rice, cranberry and savory mushrooms and that makes for a healthy main course with a presentation that is nothing less than 5-star gourmet. Whether you are cooking for family or guests, this dish is sure to delight.

1/2 cup chopped Celery
1/4 cup sliced fresh Mushrooms
2 tablespoons Butter
6 oz. fast-cooking long grain and wild Rice mix (made with chicken broth instead of water)
1/2 cup sliced Water Chestnuts, chopped
1/2 cup dried Cranberries
1/2 cup chopped Green Onions

In a large saucepan, cook the celery and mushrooms in the butter until just tender. Add in the rice and stir to coat, cooking 1 minute more. Stir in the appropriate amount of chicken broth (according to rice package directions). Bring to a boil, then reduce heat, cover and simmer until rice is tender.
Stir in the water chestnuts, cranberries, onions and soy sauce. Mix well. Stuff this mixture into the hens. Arrange the hens on the tall rack of the SuperWave and bake at 375° for 30 minutes or until the juices run clear and a meat thermometer inserted into stuffing reads 165°. Cut each hen in half lengthwise to serve.

Nut-Crusted Chicken Breasts
With Mustard Sauce

PREP: 20 minutes COOK: 10-12 minutes SERVES: 4

The wonderful thing we've found about the SuperWave Oven is that it makes fancy dishes easy to prepare. One of the concerns of any crusted meat is that the crust can get overcooked before the meat is done. Thanks to the infrared element that cooks the meat from the inside out, along with the SuperWave's convection heating, the crust ends up a golden brown just as the meat is tender, juicy and finished to perfection.

4 small to medium boneless, skinless Chicken Breasts
5 TBS unsalted Butter, melted
4 TBS Dijon Mustard
½ cup finely chopped Walnuts
salt and freshly ground Pepper to taste
½ cup plain Yogurt
2 TBS Mayonnaise

Place each chicken breast between 2 piec of wax paper and pound lightly with a wooden mallet or the back of a large serving spoon until about 1/4" to 3/8" thick. Set aside.

In a bowl large enough to accommodate one of the breasts, whisk together the melted butter and 2 TBS of the mustard. Place the chopped walnuts in a second bowl of similar size. Dip each piece of the chicken in the butter/mustard mix first, then in the walnuts. Coat the chicken well with the nuts Sprinkle with a little salt and pepper to taste.

Place the breasts on the top rack of the SuperWave and bake at 375° for 10-12 minutes.

Just before serving, whisk together the yogurt, mayonnaise, remaining mustard, and the honey in a small saucepan. Heat thoroughly, but don't boil. To serve, place a tablespoon of the sauce on each plate and swirl around. Place a chicken breast on the sauce, then drizzle with a bit more sauce. Ser immediately.

WHOLE MEAL IDEA: In a bowl, mix about 20 Green Beans with ½ an onion, minced, and a tablespoon of olive oil. Sprinkle with a little salt and pepper to taste. Place the beans and onions in small oven-safe dish on the bottom rack of the SuperWave, across the tines, so they don't fall through. Roast with the chicken breasts.

Honey Mustard Sauce

6 TBS Honey
¼ cup Dijon Mustard
Ground Red Pepper to taste

Mix ingredients together well. Refrigerate, covered for up to a month.

Hawaiian Shish Kabobs

PREP TIME: 15 minutes   COOK TIME: 10 minutes   SERVES: 4

Mom and Dad loved Hawaii. Dad had passed through there on his way to the South Pacific in WWII and Mom met him there upon his return from that duty. Years later, we kids watched as they celebrated their wedding anniversary by playing Don Ho records, holding hands, and talking softly. Only they knew the relief the relief that Hawaii meant to them and how those island sounds represented a future assured in the face of war. It seems like every year about that time, we would have this dish. It was always especially delicious.

¾ pound Chicken Breast, boneless, skinless
8 skewers
1 Red Onion, cut in wedges
1 Red Pepper, large slices
1 fresh Pineapple, chunks
8 Cherry Tomatoes
½ cup Oil
½ cup Soy Sauce
3 TBS each Hoisin Sauce, Sherry and Brown Sugar
½ tsp Ginger, ground
2 cloves Garlic, minced

Cut chicken into 1 inch cubes. Arrange vegetables and chicken on skewers ending with 1 cherry tomato on each. Place in a shallow glass dish. In a small glass bowl whisk together oil, soy sauce, hoisin sauce, sherry, brown sugar, ginger, and garlic. Pour this over chicken kabobs. Marinate 10 minutes.

Spray upper rack with nonstick cooking spray. Place the kabobs on the rack. Cook at 350°F for 10 minutes.

Green Chili Enchiladas

PREP: 15 minutes   COOK: 15 minutes   SERVES: 4

Back in the days when we worked together at The Crepe Chalet, we often had workers from around the world pass through our doors as line or prep cooks. This recipe comes to us via one young Mexican immigrant named Jorge.
While he used pulled pork in the original, the ground turkey here makes for a much healthier dish.

½ pound Ground Turkey
1 medium Onion, chopped
4 Green Onions, chopped
2 Chipotle Peppers, minced
1 Pkg Flour Tortillas
1 can Black Refried Beans
1 can sliced Water Chestnuts
1 can Green Chili Enchilada Sauce
8 oz Cheddar Cheese, grated

In a large skillet over medium-high heat, brown the turkey with the onions and chipotle peppers. Remove from heat and chop the meat fine and set aside.

Smear a flour tortilla with black refried beans, then add in 3-4 tablespoons of the turkey and onion mixture. Top with a few water chestnuts and sprinkle the cheese along the length of the tortilla. Spoon on a tablespoon or two of the Enchilada Sauce. Roll up into an enchilada about ¾" in diameter and lay in an 8" or 10" baking dish, seam side down. Repeat this procedure until the dish is filled.

Cover the top of the enchiladas with a little more of the sauce and a healthy sprinkling of the grated cheese.

Place the dish on the bottom rack of the SuperWave and bake for 15 minutes at 350º.
Serve with a dollop of sour cream.

Duck Breasts with Balsamic-Onion Marmalade

PREP: 5 minutes (duck) COOK: 8-10 minutes (duck) SERVES: 4

Duck has always been one of our favorite dishes, but it's always been a little temperamental in that it can dry out so easily in a conventional oven, and unless you have a great sauce, it kind of misses the mark. But because of the way the SuperWave cooks, these breasts come out moist and tender, and the Marmalade we offer here is spectacular with them.

4 Duck Breast Halves- Skin On
**   Salt and freshly ground pepper**

Preheat oven to 400° F.

Score each breast shallowly in a crisscross fashion. Do NOT slice into the meat. These cuts allow the fat to render and the skin to get crispy.

Sprinkle each breast on both sides with salt and pepper. You can be generous with the salt on the skin side. It really helps dry out the skin so you get a super crispy skin.

Place duck breasts skin side up on the tall rack of the SuperWave and cook for about 3 minutes or until the skin is golden brown. Remember to watch it carefully -- you want to crisp the skin, but not overcook the meat. You might have to lower the temperature a bit. Patience is the main ingredient for a perfect duck breast, and each one is going to be a little different.

Turn the duck breasts over and continue to cook for another 4-5 minutes or until Medium Rare (130-135°). Remember -- watch your duck carefully because cooking time varies on how thick your breasts are and how much has already cooked through when you seared them. They will also continue to cook a little once you remove the breasts from the oven.

While the breasts are roasting, make the Balsamic Onion Marmalade.

Remove the breasts to a warm plate skin side up and let rest for 5 to 10 minutes and then slice about 1/2 inch thick on the diagonal and serve with the Balsamic Onion Marmalade.

Balsamic-Onion Marmalade

PREP: 5 minutes COOK: 15 minutes MAKES about 2 cups

2 large Red Onions (about 1 1/4 lbs)
**   thinly sliced**
3 TBS Brown Sugar
3/4 cup dry Red Wine
3 TBS Balsamic Vinegar

In a heavy pan, combine the onions and brown sugar over medium-high heat, stirring often, until the onions are soft and just beginning to caramelize.

Stir in the wine and vinegar. Increase the heat, and continue stirring, until the sauce has thickened a bit. Season to taste with salt and pepper and spoon over the breasts when ready to serve.

Raspberry Glazed Chicken

PREP: 3 minutes   COOK: 8 minutes   SERVES: 4

The beauty of this whole meal combination is that it exemplifies what the SuperWave Oven does best. Healthy food made quickly and loaded with flavor. This low fat meal unites lean protein with the nutritional benefits of quinoa (pronounced keen-wah), a supergrain from the Andes which has the perfect balance of amino acids for humans. Everything a healthy body needs in less than 15 minutes start to finish.

½ cup Raspberry Jam
1 TBS Dijon Mustard
4 Chicken Breasts

Blend the jam with the mustard and brush on each chicken breast, top and bottom.

Place on the top rack in the SuperWave and bake at 350º for 8 minutes.
Serve with Rosemary Quinoa.

ROSEMARY QUINOA

PREP: 2 minutes   COOK: 8 minutes

1 cup Quinoa
2 cups water
1 clove Garlic, crushed
½ tsp Salt
1 TBS fresh Rosemary, minced

Mix all ingredients together and place in a bowl on the bottom rack of the SuperWave and cook along with the chicken.

Curry Rubbed Hens or Chicken

PREP: 5 minutes   COOK: 25 minutes (hens)   SERVES: 4
35 minutes. (chicken)

In 1996, we met a gentleman from Kerala, India who was a Doctor of alternative healing known as Ayurveda. In Ayurveda, the entire cure for ones ailments is met through proper diet. The following recipe is proof that treatment can be delicious. Our friend tells us that this recipe is good as a general tonic for well-being, turmeric being of particular benefit to digestion. The couscous side dish is meant to prevent hyperacidity. To health!

**2 Cornish Game Hens or 1 Whole Chicken
  (4-5 pounds)
1 TBS Olive Oil
2 TBS Curry
1 TBS Cumin, ground
1 TBS Cumin Seed, whole
½ TBS Turmeric, ground
½ tsp Salt
1 TBS ground Mustard**

Mix spices and oil thoroughly, then rub over poultry, being sure to rub the mix in the cavity. Place on bottom rack in the SuperWave and bake at 375º for 25 minutes.

To make the meal, prepare Coconut Cilantro Couscous (page 122) during the last 10 minutes of cooking the bird(s).

Beef

London Broil (with a Cabernet Reduction Sauce)

PREP TIME: 20 minutes   COOK TIME: 10-12 minutes for medium (fresh)   SERVES: 4-6
14-16 minutes for medium (frozen)

London broil is one of the least appreciated cuts on the cow, even though it is one of the most flavorful. Because of this, you can often get them on sale at your local market. Buy in bulk and freeze the extra meat in a freezer bag along with this marinade. When you are ready to enjoy it, put it right in the SuperWave to cook from frozen. You won't believe the flavor or the ease of preparation.

1 2-pound London Broil
¼ cup Oil
¼ cup Water
1 clove Garlic, finely minced
1 teaspoon Salt

In a glass bowl, whisk together the oil, water, garlic, and salt. Place meat in a shallow glass dish, pour marinade over beef. Marinate15 minutes. Spray lower rack with non stick cooking spray. Place beef on rack. Cook at 325° for 10-12 minutes for medium.

Cabernet Reduction Sauce

1 TBS Oil
2 TBS minced Shallot
2 TBS minced Garlic
2/3 bottle dry Cabernet
3 cups Beef Stock
2 Bay Leaves
1 sprig Rosemary
3 TBS Dijon Mustard
3 TBS Worchestershire Sauce
½ cup sliced Mushrooms (optional)

PREP: 10 minutes COOK: 20 minutes MAKES 1 cup

Place all ingredients in a saucepan. Reduce at a simmer over medium-low heat until thick and syrupy, approximately 20 minutes. If using the mushrooms, add them in after the reduction.

WHOLE MEAL IDEA: Prepare the Roasted Asparagus recipe (page 122) and place the asparagus across half the tines of the bottom rack. On the other half of the bottom rack, place ¼" thick slices of baking potato (skin washed and left on), on which you have sprinkled a little salt and pepper. Roast with the London Broil. Serve the potatoes with a dollop of Sour Cream.

Deviled Hamburgers

PREP: 15 minutes   COOK: 10 minutes   MAKES: 4

A hamburger is a hamburger is a hamburger. At least it was until Mom went home to visit her parents and Dad took over the cooking. He was a culinary adventurer, was our father, and we never knew what might end up on our plates. What follows is one of the Dad's triumphs. We liked these so much we even ended up having them when Mom was around. We called them "Daddy Burgers" to distinguish them from patties of lesser provenance.

1 pound ground Beef
1/3 cup Chili Sauce
1 ½ TBS Horseradish
1 tsp chopped Onion
1 ½ tsp prepared Mustard
1 ½ tsp Worcestershire Sauce
1 tsp Salt
   dash of Pepper
4 Hamburger Buns
   melted Butter

Combine all ingredients in a bowl and mix thoroughly.
Cut the buns in half. Place a mound of the meat mix on each half. Brush with the melted butter. Broil on the top rack of the SuperWave until cooked through, about 5 minutes per side for medium.

WHOLE MEAL IDEA: Cut a baking potato into 1/8" square shoestring slices, sprinkle with salt to taste, and place across the bottom rack of the SuperWave while the hamburgers are cooking. Nothing like a burger and fries.

Mustard-Crusted Flank Steak

PREP: 5 minutes   COOK: 10 minutes (fresh)   SERVES: 4
                             14 minutes (frozen)

Yellow mustard sometimes gets relegated to hot dogs and ham sandwiches. That's a shame. Properly applied to meat, yellow mustard is the chameleon of spices. In this recipe, as the steak cooks, it browns the mustard and transforms it into something else entirely. The mustard becomes that unidentifiable ingredient that pulls it all together and will have your guests or family guessing what magic you have employed to delight them. Let 'em guess. You know the secret now.

4 TBS Butter
1 TBS Olive Oil
3 TBS Shallots, minced
1 TBS Thyme
½ tsp Black Pepper, course ground
½ tsp Red Pepper, crushed
4 TBS Yellow Mustard
1 pounds Flank Steak

Mix the first six ingredients into a paste and rub it onto the flank steak, top and bottom.

Broil at 480° on the top rack of the SuperWave for 5 minutes on each side for medium rare. Let stand 2 minutes before slicing and serving.

WHOLE MEAL IDEA: Slice a small to medium onion into ¼" thick rounds and place the center cuts on the bottom rack of the SuperWave. Top with large florets of Broccoli and a pat of butter on each. Let bake while the Flank Steak is broiling.

Stuffed Peppers

PREP TIME: 20 minutes   COOK TIME: 35 minutes   SERVES: 5

Dad was an avid gardener. For most of the summer, Saturday mornings were Dad's time to spend with his boys, and that meant planting, weeding, and cultivating our jam-packed garden. Looking back on it, it was absolutely amazing the amount of fresh produce we squeezed out of that half acre and the fun we had doing it. One of the things we harvested in abundance were bell peppers of every color. When the bounty came in, Mom would prepare them like this and freeze them. That way, we could bring back the taste of summer even o cold February days. Give it a try. The SuperWave will cook them from frozen so th peppers still have that fresh-picked crunch.

5 Bell Peppers
1 cup Rice, cooked
¾ pound Ground Beef
1 TBS Olive Oil
1 small Onion, chopped
1 rib Celery, minced
2 cloves Garlic, minced
1 tsp dried Oregano
1 TBS fresh Basil, minced (1 tsp dried)
1 cup plus 5 TBS Tomato Sauce

In a medium pan, sauté ground beef until brown.
While beef is cooking cut the tops off the peppers, dice the tops, and set them aside.
Remove the seeds and membranes from the pepper cavities.
When the beef is browned, drain the grease and place the meat into a bowl. In the same pan you browned the beef in, add the olive oil, then add the onions, celery, garlic, and chopped pepper tops. Saute for 2 minutes. Add the oregano, basil, and tomato sauce and stir 1 minute longer
In a large bowl, combine the meat mixture and the cooked rice. Fluff this together well. Stuff peppers with this filling.
Spray lower rack with non stick cooking spray. Arrange the shorter peppers on this rack. Use the extender ring and place the taller peppers on the top rack. Top each pepper with 1 tablespoon of tomato sauce. Cook at 350° for 35 minutes.

Black Bean Chili Cups
with Chipotle Cornbread Topping

PREP: 10 minutes   COOK: 8–10 minutes   SERVES: 6

There's nothing we like better than a presentation that looks like it took a feat of engineering, but was so easy a child could do it. Well, here it is. Nothing goes better with chili than cornbread, and nothing goes better with black bean chili than chipotle cornbread. The servings are portion controlled and everybody gets "the good slice" of cornbread. We love it when a plan comes together!

1 pound lean Ground Beef
3 slices Bacon, chopped
1 medium Onion
2 cloves Garlic, minced
1 can Black Beans, rinsed
1 can Stewed Tomatoes
1 TBS Cumin
2 TBS Chili Powder
Salt and Pepper

Place the ground beef, bacon, onions and garlic in a 10" round casserole dish and brown on the top rack in the SuperWave Oven at 450° for 5 minutes. Remove from the oven and pour into a bowl and mince.

Stir in the beans, tomatoes and spices. Let sit for 5 minutes. Ladle the mixture into ramekins (filling them about ¾ of the way), and then top with the Chipotle Cornbread batter. Bake on the lower rack in the SuperWave for 8 minutes at 400°.

Chipotle Cornbread

PREP: 5 minutes   COOK: 8–10 minutes   SERVES: 8

We know this goes with the chili, but if you want to make a pan of this, no one is going to complain. Believe us.

1 cup Corn Meal
1 cup Flour
¼ cup Sugar
3 tsp Baking Powder
1 tsp Salt
¼ cup Butter, melted
1 cup milk
1 Egg, beaten
2 Chipotle Peppers, minced

Combine the corn meal, flour, sugar, baking powder, peppers and salt in a bowl.
Mix the butter, egg, and milk together in a separate bowl, then add to the dry ingredients.
Spoon on top of the chili ramekins for chili cups or bake in a shallow 8" nonstick cake pan on the top rack of the SuperWave for 10 minutes at 400°. Corn bread may cook more quickly, so remove when golden brown.

Aunt Noni's Meatballs

With Mary's 10-Minute Marinara and Crusty Garlic Bread

PREP: 12 minutes   COOK: 14 minutes (fresh)   MAKES: 20 meatballs
                              16-18 minutes (from frozen)

Noni was an ancient Italian woman who sat for us when we were small (which means she was probably all of 50 years old when we made that judgment). She could cook like an angel and took care of us as if we were her own. Her meatballs are the best you will ever taste. Don't skimp on the garlic!

1 slice White Bread
½ cup Milk
1 pound lean ground Beef
1/2 medium Onion
4 TBS Parmesan Cheese
2 TBS Ricotta Cheese
1 Egg, jumbo
4 cloves Garlic, crushed
¼ tsp Cayenne Pepper
¼ cup Italian Parsley, chopped fine
** Pinch Nutmeg**
** Salt and Pepper to taste**
1 TBS Olive Oil
** Italian Seasoned Breadcrumbs, as needed**

In a large bowl, soak the bread in the milk until absorbed. Add the raw beef, onion, cheeses, egg, spices, herbs and oil and mix thoroughly. Add breadcrumbs as needed to bind the mixture together (but don't use too much, or the meatballs will be dry). Shape into 1-1/2" balls by rolling a small handful of the mixture in the palms. Roll the balls in a bowl of the breadcrumbs to just barely coat and place on the bottom rack of the SuperWave. Bake at 400° for 14 minutes or until browned and fragrant.

Great Combo: Serve with Mary's Ten-Minute Marinara and Crusty Garlic Bread (page 47).

TIP: These are great to make ahead and freeze. When freezing, place in a a ziplock freezer bag in one layer, and lay flat on a shelf in the freezer. They'll be fine in the freezer for up to 3months. Since the SuperWave is super with cooking from frozen, just cook the frozen meatballs as directed but don't forget to adjust the time.

Mary's Ten-Minute Marinara

PREP: 3 minutes   COOK: 7–10 minutes   MAKES: 3 Cups

This sounds too easy to be real, but try it. You won't be sorry. It renders a sauce that is slightly sweet and so good you'll want to lick the plate.

2 pounds Cherry Tomatoes
2 TBS Olive Oil
10 fresh Basil leaves, hand torn into pieces
6 cloves Garlic, peeled and sliced
   Sea Salt and coarse ground Pepper
   Grated Parmesan

In a bowl, toss the cherry tomatoes, garlic, basil, salt and pepper with olive oil.
Spread in a single layer on a 10" round baking sheet or plate in the SuperWave Oven. Broil at 425° for 7-10 minutes.

Crusty Garlic Bread

10 slices Italian Bread, sliced ½" thick
5 cloves Garlic, peeled and halved

Place bread on the top rack in the SuperWave Oven and broil until toasted at 450°.
While the bread is still very hot, remove it from the SuperWave and immediately rub each slice with half a garlic clove. The garlic will literally melt onto the bread! It's a delicious way to get a side dish with no added fat!

Steak Fajitas

PREP: 20 minutes (not counting marinating) COOK: 10 minutes SERVES: 4

Maybe it's because they're so easy to make. Or maybe it's that the kids love that they get to get their hands into their food and put what they want in the tortilla. Or maybe it's that we love the fact that you can use just about anything you have leftover in the fridge to make them. We used flank steak here, but honestly, you can use any cut of beef.. Or for that matter, chicken, pork, or even fish!

Marinade:
   Juice of 1 Lime
   2 Tablespoons of Olive Oil
   2 cloves Garlic, peeled, minced
   1/2 teaspoon ground Cumin
   1/2 fresh Jalapeño Pepper, seeded,
      finely chopped
   1/4 cup chopped fresh Cilantro, including
      stems

Fajitas:
   1 lb of Flank Steak or Skirt Steak, cut against
      the grain into thin slices
   1 large Yellow Onion, peeled and sliced into
      ½" rings, then the rings cut in half
   2 large Bell Peppers, stemmed, seeded,
      and sliced lengthwise into half-inch wide strips
   1 cup shredded Cheese (Monterey Jack is good)
   1-1 ½ cups shredded Iceberg Lettuce
      Sour Cream or Guacamole
   6-8 Flour Tortillas

Mix all marinade ingredients. Set the steak in the marinade and let it sit at least an hour, the longer the better. In a shallow, 10" round baking dish or cake pan, place the steak and all the other ingredients except the tortillas, cheese, lettuce, sour cream or guacamole. Spread them evenly in the pan. Place the pan on the tall rack of the SuperWave and roast at 300° for about 5 minutes. Turn all the ingredients in the pan (with tongs or a spatula) and roast again for another 5 minutes or until the steak is medium-rare to medium, and the vegetables are crisp-tender.
If you'd like, you can stack the tortillas on the lower rack while the above is roasting, to warm them.

When the meat and vegetable are done, remove the pan and tortillas and serve with the shredded cheese, salsa, shredded iceberg lettuce, sour cream, and guacamole.

Workingman's Wellington

PREP: 5 minutes   COOK: 12 minutes (fresh)   SERVES: 2

We love surprises, especially when it comes to food. That's why we enjoy "hidden treasure" presentations. What is going to be eaten is not known until that first bite, so you want to make that first bite count. This dish provides elegance and haute cuisine without the hassle or pretense. On top of that, it is absolutely delicious and maintains that delight with each and every bite.

6 Crimini Mushrooms, sliced
1 can refrigerated Crescent Dough
2 TBS Sherry, Brandy or Madeira
2 TBS Butter
  Garlic Powder, Salt, and Pepper to taste
2 (4-6 oz) Rib Eye Steaks
1 recipe Chicken Liver Pate, (in a pinch, slices of Liverwurst work nicely here

Place the mushrooms in an oven safe bowl along with the sherry, butter, salt and pepper. Cook in the SuperWave at 400° for 5 minutes, or until mushrooms have reduced. Meanwhile, rub the steaks with the garlic powder, salt, and pepper to taste, or some other seasoning of your choice.

Divide the dough into 4 rectangles, ignoring the corner-to-corner perforations. Place each steak on a rectangle, spread with pate, and spoon the mushroom reduction over top. Fold dough corners up and seal at the top, pinching the sides to conform to the shape of the steak. Place the wrapped steaks on the bottom rack of the SuperWave and bake at 400° for 10-12 minutes for a medium steak.

Drunken Brisket

PREP: 8 minutes (not counting marinating)   COOK: 14 minutes   SERVES: 6-8

While this recipe calls for brisket, we want to take this opportunity to recommend you try it with the flatiron roast. The flatiron cut is virtually unknown in American cuisine, but is considered to be the second most tender cut of beef after the filet. Often referred to as the oyster blade steak, it lends itself particularly well to cooking in the SuperWave Oven. Try it. You may have just found your new favorite cut of beef.

3 TBS Olive Oil
2 TBS Dijon Mustard
¼ cup Bourbon Whiskey
1/3 cup Soy Sauce
2 TBS Red Wine Vinegar
1 TBS Worcestershire Sauce
¼ cup Dark Brown Sugar
2 TBS Red Onion, minced
1 TBS Garlic, minced
1 TBS fresh Ginger, minced
1 TBS Salt
2 TSP Black Pepper, course ground
1 (2-3 pound) Brisket or Flatiron Roast

In a medium bowl, mix all the ingredients except the brisket. Place the brisket in a zip-lock bag and add the marinade mixture. Refrigerate and allow to marinate for 24 hours. Shake the bag or turn the steak occasionally.

Broil the marinated brisket on the tall rack in the SuperWave at 480° for 7 minutes per side for medium. Slice thin and serve.

Grandma's Classic Meat Loaf

PREP: 15 minutes   COOK: 30–35 minutes   MAKES: one meat loaf

This is old-school cooking at its best. Back in the day, our Grandmother did whatever was necessary to stretch the meat. One of the ways she employed to do that was to increase flavor whil pumping up the volume. By blending the earthiness of beef with the sweetness of veal and the spiciness of pork, Grandma delivered the flavor. The other ingredients here allowed her to deliver the volume to a hungry family as well. We share this so you can do the same.

1 pound Ground Beef
1 pound Ground Veal
1 pound Ground Pork
1 tsp Baking Powder
1 small Onion, chopped
¼ cup Celery, chopped
2 tsp Salt
2 slices Bread
½ cup Catsup
1 Egg
½ cup Tomato Juice
1 Mango, sliced thinly

Mix all the ingredients except the mango without overmixing. Form into a loaf and place in a loaf pan.

Bake on the lower rack of the SuperWave at 375º for about 30-35 minutes. For the last 5-8 minutes of the baking, place the mango slices across the top of the meat loaf.

Variations: The meat loaf can be topped with a tomato-paste for a more authentic look and taste. You might also try adding a steak sauce as the topping, with some chopped mushrooms included. Add the sauces about 10 minutes before the meat loaf is finished cooking.

Filet Stuffed with Oysters and Prosciutto

PREP: 15 minutes   COOK: 13 minutes (medium well)   SERVES: 4

The fine 19th Century tradition of cooking beef with oysters was never part of our upbringing. That was a crying shame. We found a skeleton of this recipe in an old cookbook from the gold rush era in California. We update it here with tarragon and prosciutto to punch up the flavor and make it just about perfect.

4 TBS Butter
2 oz Prosciutto, sliced into narrow strips
2 cloves Garlic, minced
2 Green Onions, chopped fine
1 ½ pounds shucked Oysters
1 tsp fresh Tarragon
1 tsp Worcestershire Sauce
1 (10 oz) PKG frozen Spinach, thawed and squeezed dry
1 cup soft Breadcrumbs
Salt and Pepper to taste
2 pound Fillet of Beef, rubbed with Thyme and Garlic Paste

Melt the butter in a medium skillet over medium heat. Put in the prosciutto and the garlic and toss for a minute.

Add the green onions, along with the oyster and their liquor, the tarragon, and Worcestershire sauce. Cook until the oyster begin to plump. Transfer the oyster mixture and any liquid in the pan to a bowl and add the spinach.

Gently stir in just enough bread crumbs to bind the stuffing; it should still be moist. Adjust the salt and pepper.

Butterfly the fillet of beef and stuff with the oyster mix. Tie the roast together in several places wit string. Brush with olive oil and place on the low rack in the SuperWave. Roast for 6 minutes at 450°, then turn and roast for another 7 for medium well.

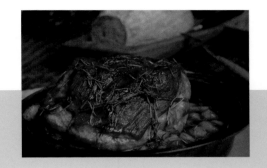

Pork and Lamb

Baked Chops Stuffed with Mincemeat

PREP: 20 minutes (including mincemeat)   COOK: 30 minutes   SERVES: 6

Few meats lend themselves to being "fruited" better than pork. The mincemeat in this recipe tastes just like a spiced apple. Now we understand why whole roasted pig is always served with an apple in its mouth. They just go so well together!

6 1-1½" Shoulder Chops
   Salt and Pepper to taste

Cut a pocket into each chop along the longitudinal line. Make sure the slice goes all the way to the bone, but not through the other side. Stuff each chop with 2-3 tablespoons of the mincemeat.

Bake at 350° for 15 minutes, then turn the chops. Bake another 15 minutes at 350° or until internal temperature reaches 160-165°.

MinceMeat

PREP: 10 minutes   COOK: 10 minutes   MAKES: about 2 cups

½ pound butter
1 box Currants
2 tsp ground Cinnamon
2 boxes seeded Raisins
½ Citron, cut fine
½ gallon Sweet Cider
3 cups Apples, chopped
1 tsp ground Nutmeg
1 tsp ground Cloves
1 tsp ground Allspice
¼ cup Brown Sugar

Not only is this a great stuffing, but it also makes a terrific pie filling!

Add all ingredients together and mix well. Bring to a boil and cook until syrupy.
Mincemeat can be used for stuffing or for a topping on meats like pork. Can be refrigerated for up to two weeks.

Pork Roast with Garlic And Rosemary

PREP TIME: 5 minutes   COOK TIME: 60 minutes   SERVES: 6

This is one of those dishes that fills your home with such delicious aromas that your family's mouths will be watering from the moment they step into the house. It grew out of our mother's love of rosemary and our father's obsession with garlic...a perfect marriage in our estimation. See what you and your family think.

1 2-3-pound Pork Roast
2 TBS Olive Oil
1 TBS Lemon Juice, fresh
3 cloves Garlic, sliced
1 tsp Salt
½ tsp Pepper
2 TBS Rosemary, fresh, chopped

In a small bowl mix olive oil and lemon juice.
Make 6 to 8 cuts into the pork with sharp knife. Tuck garlic into the cut. Brush oil and lemon mixture over pork. Sprinkle with salt, pepper and rosemary.
Spray the lower rack with nonstick cooking spray. Place the roast on the rack. Cook at 350° for 60 minutes or until thermometer reads 160°.
Remove roast when done and let rest 15 minutes before cutting.

<u>WHOLE MEAL IDEA</u>: *Surround the pork roast with 2 cups of Brussels Sprouts and 2 cups of Baby Carrots. Squeeze the juice of 1 lemon over them. By the time the Pork is cooked through, the vegetables will be just right.*

Apple and Onion Pork Chops

PREP: 7 minutes   COOK: 20 minutes   SERVES: 4

Every dinner we had growing up had applesauce to go with it. It was a German tradition from our father's side of the family. These days, being older and more careful about what we eat, we look for opportunities to include fresh fruit without additives like high fructose corn syrup. This dish is perfect. Sweet and savory, healthy fruit, good meat protein, and loads of flavor!

4 Pork Chops, ½" thick
   Lawry's or Monterey Seasoned Salt
2 firm Red Apples, peeled, cored, halved, and sliced ¼" thick
1 Onion, peeled and sliced ¼" thick
1 TBS Honey

Rub the chops with the seasoned salt and sear on one side at 480° for 1-2 minutes on the top rack of the SuperWave. Turn and sear the other side for about 1-2 minutes. Remove the lid and the rack of chops.

WHOLE MEAL IDEA: *Place the onions in a layer on the bottom rack of the SuperWave. Place the apple slices on top of the onion slices. Return the chops rack to the SuperWave and bake at 350° for 15 minutes, or until pork temperature is 160-165° (for medium), allowing the juices to drip onto the apples and onions.*

Lamb Chops With Mint

PREP TIME: 5 minutes (not including marinating)   COOK TIME: 25 minutes   SERVES: 4

When we were growing up, Mom would serve us lamb smothered in super sweet mint jelly. While that contributed to our appreciation of mint jelly, it did little to help us appreciate the succulence of properly cooked lamb. The SuperWave Oven amply provides that opportunity by roasting the meat to perfection as the sweet and savory marinade provides the touches of garlic and mint that make lamb sing.

4 Loin or Bone-in Lamb Chops,
  no more than 1" thick
1 clove Garlic, minced
½ tsp Salt
¼ tsp Pepper
1½ tsp Sugar
¼ cup Olive Oil
½ cup Red Wine Vinegar
½ cup Mint leaves, fresh, minced

In a small bowl whisk together garlic, olive oil, salt, pepper, sugar, vinegar, and mint leaves.

In a shallow glass dish place chops, pour marinade over chops. Cover and marinate 30 minutes.

Spray upper rack with nonstick cooking spray and place in unit. Lay the chops on the rack. Brush with the marinade.

Cook for 15 minutes at 375º. Open the lid, turn the chops, and brush a little more marinade on them. Continue to cook another 10 minutes or until cooked as desired.

Pineapple Glazed Ham

PREP TIME: 5 minutes   COOK TIME: 30 minutes   SERVES: 4

Mom was a traditional southern cook and that meant Sunday dinner tables stacked high with foods like all-day beans, great messes of cooked greens, scalloped potatoes, slaw, biscuits and this dish. It was always our job to "pin" the whole cloves into the ham. That was fine with us. We'd pocket a few choice cloves to chew on later.

2 pound cooked Ham
1 8-ounce can sliced Pineapples, drained, liquid reserved
whole cloves
maraschino cherries
1 TBS Lemon juice
2 TBS Brown Sugar
1 tsp Cinnamon
1 TBS Cornstarch

Using a sharp pointed knife, score top of ham in a diamond pattern. Arrange pineapple slices on top securing with whole cloves. Place cherries in center of pineapples.

In a small pan add reserved pineapple juice, lemon juice, brown sugar, cinnamon, and cornstarch. Blend well. Stir over medium heat until glaze thickens. Remove from heat and add butter.

Spray lower rack with nonstick cooking spray. Place the ham on the rack and brush with the glaze.

Bake at 325° for 30 minutes.

Smoked Ham Cups

PREP: 20 minutes   COOK: 15-20 minutes   MAKES: 10 cups

These cups are simple, satisfying, and make for a delicious main course. We always are sure to make extra in a loaf pan on the side because, sliced and fried, this makes a great breakfast meat to serve with eggs and toast the next morning.

1 pound ground, smoked Ham (great for leftover ham)
½ pound ground fresh Pork
1 ½ cups Bread Crumbs
1 Egg, beaten
¼ cup Brown Sugar
1 tsp prepared Mustard (Dijon is fine)

Combine the ham, pork, bread crumbs, egg, and mustard in a bowl. Mix well. Fill small, individual muffin-sized casseroles with the mixture, rounding the tops as you would a meat loaf.

Combine the brown sugar and prepared mustard, and spread over the tops of the individual casserole cups.

Bake at 350° for about 15-20 minutes. Serve with Honey Mustard Sauce (page 29) or canned cherry pie filling.

Tip: Experiment with the flavors of these wonderful cups by trying different mustards with them. There are dozens of fabulous mustards available, particularly in specialty food shops. A champagne mustard, for instance, lends the perfect note of sweetness to the cups.

Roasted Pork with 50 Garlic Cloves

PREP: 15 minutes   COOK: 40 minutes   SERVES: 6-8

We know, we know. This sounds like overkill, but trust us. This much garlic gives the roast character, infusing it through and through with aromatic flavor. In return, the juices from the meat roast the garlic, turning it into an incomparable bread spread. On the page this looks like a lot, on the table, it's just barely enough. It's that good.

2 pound netted or tied Pork Shoulder Roast
2 TBS Olive Oil
½ cup White Wine, dry
½ cup Chicken Stock
50 cloves Garlic
1 tsp fresh Rosemary, chopped
½ tsp Sage, dried
Salt and Pepper
Hard-crusted bread

In a large skillet over medium-high heat, brown the pork roast in the olive oil. Transfer this to a 10" round casserole dish. Deglaze the skillet with the wine and stock. Reserve about a 1/4 cup of this sauce, then pour the rest over the roast. Scatter the garlic cloves and herbs around the roast in the casserole. Bake on the lower rack of the SuperWave at 350° for 40 minutes. Baste the roast every 10 minutes or so with the reserved sauce, to keep it moist and concentrate the flavors. To serve, slice the pork and spoon over with the garlic.

Tip: A great way to get everything out of this dish is to serve it with a good, hard-crusted bread. Use the garlic cloves as a spread for the bread (instead of butter). The cloves will be soft and spreadable, and the flavor is spectacular!

Sweet Barbecue Pork Shoulder

PREP: 15 minutes   COOK: 30 minutes   SERVES: 6

Pork shoulder is a particularly well-marbled cut, lending itself to recipes that revel in juicy, tender, flavorful presentations. There are few more delicious cuts and, by our estimation, that has barbeque written all over it. The sauce we offer here has all the sweet tang and deep notes that will do such fine meat justice.

1 cup of Ketchup
¼ cup of Apple Juice
¼ cup of Apple Cider Vinegar
¼ cup of Worcestershire Sauce or Soy Sauce
1 teaspoon of Garlic Powder, a small amount of grated Apple
1 tsp grated Onion
1 tsp grated Green Pepper
Pepper to taste.

To make the sauce, place the first 8 ingredients in a saucepan over medium heat and stir to blend. Simmer until slightly thickened.

Spray the top rack of the SuperWave with nonstick cooking spray. Season the chops with the salt and pepper to taste, and place on the rack. Brush the chops liberally with the sauce.

Bake at 350º for 15 minutes, then turn the chops, again brushing them liberally with the sauce.

Bake another 15 minutes at 350º or until internal temperature of the chops reaches 150-165 degrees.

Baby Back Ribs in a Hot Sweet Whiskey Sauce

PREP: 90 minutes COOK: 2-3 hours MAKES: 4 half-racks

There are as many recipes for Baby Backs as there are lovers of them. And we've never met an aficionado of these luscious ribs who didn't give the sauce their own special touch. Here's a reci Bob came across in Tennessee while on his "In The Kitchen with Bob" tour. It's a very special sauce, blending the heat of pepper, the sweet of honey, and the kick of a good, o fashioned southern whiskey. We think you'll be calling it your own the first tim you try it.

2 slabs Baby Back Pork Ribs
Salt to taste
coarsely ground Black Pepper
1 tablespoon ground Red Chile Pepper
2 1/4 tablespoons Vegetable Oil
1/2 cup minced Onion
1 1/2 cups Water
1/2 cup Tomato Paste
1/2 cup White Vinegar
1/2 cup Brown Sugar
2 1/2 tablespoons Honey
2 tablespoons Worcestershire Sauce
2 teaspoons Salt
1/4 teaspoon coarsely ground Black Pepper
1 1/4 teaspoons Liquid Smoke flavoring
2 teaspoons Whiskey
2 teaspoons Garlic Powder
1/4 teaspoon Paprika
1/2 teaspoon Onion Powder
1 tablespoon Dark Molasses
1/2 tablespoon ground Red Chile Pepper

Cut each full rack of ribs in half, so that you have 4 half racks. Sprinkle salt and pepper (more pepper than salt), and 1 tablespoon chili pepper over meat. Wrap each half rack in aluminum foil. Place on the lower rack in the SuperWave and bake at 300° for 1-1/2 to 2 hours. Meanwhile, heat oil in a medium saucepan over medium heat. Cook and stir the onions in oil for 5 minutes. Stir in water, tomato paste, vinegar, brown sugar, honey, and Worcestershire sauce. Season with 2 teaspoons salt, 1/4 teaspoon black pepper, liquid smoke, whiskey, garlic powder, paprika, onion powder, dark molasses, and 1/2 tablespoon ground chili pepper. Bring mixture to a boil, then reduce heat. Simmer for 1 1/4 hours, uncovered, or until sauce thickens. Remove from heat, and set sauce aside.

Remove the ribs from the oven, and let stand 10 minutes. Remove the racks from the foil, and place on the top rack of the SuperWave. Grill the ribs for 3 to 4 minutes on each side. Brush the sauce liberally on the ribs while they're grilling, just before you serve them (adding it too early will burn it).

Stuffed Rolled Pork Loin

PREP: 12 minutes   COOK: 25 minutes   SERVES: 6-8

It's a dish like this that pork producers are imagining when they call pork "the other white meat" This has it all. It's lean, delicious, has a marvelous presentation and it's good for you! Serve thi at your next dinner party to impress your guests. It's a no-fail preparation that wil net you loads of compliments.

- **½ cup Almonds, sliced**
- **½ cup Craisins**
- **3 Green Onions, chopped fine**
- **1 rib Celery, minced**
- **1 Egg, beaten**
- **4 oz. Asiago Cheese, grated**
- **1 tsp Rosemary**
- **1 TBS dried Basil**
- **20 oz frozen chopped Spinach, thawed and squeezed dry**
- **1 cup cooked Rice**
- **2 cloves Garlic, minced**
- **Salt and Pepper to taste**

On an oven-safe plate or round baking sheet, toast the almonds on the top rack of the SuperWave for 5 minutes at 400°. Remove, cool and mix in a large bowl wit all other ingredients, except the pork, making sure everything is evenly blended Spread out stuffing onto pork loin in an even layer, covering entire surface of the meat. Roll up meat from one end and secure using cooking twine at the ends and the center of the roast. Roast on the lower rack in SuperWave Oven 20 minutes at 375°.

WHOLE MEAL IDEA:

Surround the rolled pork loin with small fingerling potatoes cut in half lengthwise. Nestle broccoli florets in among the potatoes, near the pork. You might want to put a quarter inch of water on the bottom of the SuperWave bowl for moisture.

Seafood

Stuffed Colossal Shrimp

PREP TIME: 20 minutes   COOK TIME: 20 minutes   SERVES: 6

Officially, there are eleven different sizes of shrimp. In our experience, larger shrimp come from warmer waters and have a rounder, more complex taste. Colossal shrimp have the texture of lobster but a sweeter, brighter flavor which does not overshadow the subtle crab notes in the stuffing here. In this case, bigger is definitely better.

3-5 Colossal Shrimp, peeled, deveined, and slit longitudinally to form a pocket
Choose either: Crabmeat mixture (see below) or Fresh Horseradish
Choose either: Prosciutto, sliced thinly or Bacon, partially cooked
Toothpicks
Juice of 1 lemon

Fill the pocket in the shrimp with either the Crabmeat mixture or the horseradish.
Wrap the stuffed shrimp with the prosciutto or the bacon. Secure with toothpicks.

Crabmeat Mixture Stuffing

2 TBS Butter
½ Onion, chopped
2 tablespoons Parsley
1 tablespoon Dill, fresh
¼ teaspoon Pepper
¼ teaspoon Salt
2 tablespoons White Wine
cup Bread Crumbs
6 ounces Crab meat
juice from 1 Lemon

In a medium sauté pan, melt butter. Add onions, cook 2 minutes. Add parsley, dill, pepper, salt, white wine, and bread crumbs. Blend well. Add crab meat and stir. Stuff the shrimp with a TBS or two of the crabmeat mix. Secure with a toothpick.

Horseradish Stuffing

1 jar hot prepared Horseradish
Several pieces Proscuitto, very thinly sliced (or Bacon, partially cooked)

Stuff the pocket in the shrimp with about 1 TBS of the horseradish (or more to taste).
Wrap the stuffed shrimp in a layer or two of the prosciutto (depending up on the proscuitto's thickness), and secure with a toothpick.
Cook as instructed above.

Seared Tuna with Doctor D Sauce and Onions

PREP: 10 minutes (not including marinating)   COOK: 12 minutes   SERVES: 4

*Years ago, Paul earned his chef chops in part under the mercurial and brilliant Denver restaurateur Perry Warren. This founder of Mostly Seafood was well ahead of his time and brought great seafood to a land-locked city. What follows is a variation on one of Perry's signature marinades. And as Perry would say: "**Don't** overcook the tuna. Medium rare is perfect."*

Doctor D Sauce:
- **¾ cup Olive Oil**
- **4 cloves Garlic, minced**
- **½ cup Red Wine Vinegar**
- **Juice of 2 fresh Lemons**
- **¼ cup Sesame Oil**
- **½ cup Soy Sauce**
- **¼ cup Cilantro, chopped**
- **2 large Red Onion, cut into rings**
- **2 pounds Tuna Steaks**

In a small bowl, mix the marinade ingredients and then pour this mixture over the tuna steaks. Allow to marinate for at least 2 hours.

Place the onion rings on the bottom rack of the SuperWave oven. Place the tuna steaks on the top rack, and sear one side at 480° for 3 minute, then turn and sear the second side for another 3 minutes. Turn again, drop the temperature to 350°, and broil for an additional 3 minutes per side.

Allow the drippings to fall onto the onions as they are caramelizing. Remove the fish to a serving platter when done, but allow the onions a few additional minutes as the fish rests before serving.

Crab Roll-Ups

PREP TIME: 15 minutes   COOK TIME: 4-5 minutes   MAKES 8

This is a nice dish that can work as an appetizer, a main course or even as tapas. It all depends on how big you make the roll-ups. Our experience has been that no matter the size, every bit of these will disappear once you make them.

1 package refrigerated Crescent Rolls
1 pound fresh lump Crab Meat,
   drained and picked
¾ cup grated Cheese (cheddar,
   Monterey Jack, or Parmesan)
2 TBS minced Onion
Salt and freshly ground Pepper to taste

Separate the individual sections of the crescent rolls and lay out on the work surface. In a glass bowl, lightly mix the crab and grated cheese.
Sprinkle each section with a little onion, salt, and pepper. Using a teaspoon, place equal amounts of the crab and cheese mixture on each of the sections, spread evenly over its area. Roll each section up, starting from the wide end.

Place the roll-ups on the high rack of the SuperWave and bake at 375° for 4-5 minutes, or until browned. Serve warm.

Mahi-Mahi with a Mango Salsa

PREP TIME: 10 minutes   COOK TIME: 10-15 minutes   SERVES: 4-6

Mahi-mahi is a wonderful fish that used to be known as dolphin-fish. Contrary to its name, it is a fairly large, finned fish not related to the intelligent mammals we know as dolphins. Because they are free swimmers, Mahi-mahi are lean and firm and their flesh is extremely sweet. The delicious salsa here helps bring that out for you to enjoy.

2-3 Mahi-Mahi fillets
4   TBS Butter, melted

Brush the Mahi fillets with the melted butter.

Place the fillets on the upper rack in the oven. Cook at 325° for 10-15 minutes or until the fish is easily flaked with the tines of a fork.

Plate the fillets and top with 2-3 tablespoons of the Mango Salsa.

Mango and Red Onion Salsa

1 large ripe Mango, peeled and cut to the 3/8" dice
1 Red Onion, finely chopped
2 Passion Fruit
6 large, fresh Basil leaves
juice of 1 Lime
Sea Salt, to taste

Place the cut mango and the chopped onion in a bowl. Halve the passion fruit and scoop out the pulp. Add to the bowl. Stack the basil leaves and trim them with scissors into 1/8" strips. Add to the bowl. Squeeze the lime juice over and mix, adding in the salt to taste. Serve immediately.

Sole Stuffed with Crabmeat

PREP TIME: 15 minutes   COOK TIME: 20 minutes   SERVES: 6

Back in the old days, fish rollup preparations were known as "fisherman's rucksacks" as they resembled the packs mariners threw together as they raced to get to their ship before it left dock. This recipe is one of countless possible variations that exist on the theme worldwide. Here, the subtle flavor of the sole plays off a mild crab sweetness that's just right.

6 Sole fillets (you can also use baby flounder)
2 TBS Butter
½ Onion, chopped
1 cup Mushrooms, chopped
2 TBS Parsley
1 TBS Dill, fresh
¼ tsp Pepper
¼ tsp Salt
2 TBS White Wine
1 cup Bread Crumbs
6 ounces Crab Meat

In a medium sauté pan, melt the butter. Add the onions and mushrooms, cook 2 minutes. Add the parsley, dill, pepper, sa white wine, and bread crumbs. Blend we Add crab meat and stir.
Divide the stuffing among the six fillets. Roll each fillet up tightly from the wider side and secure with a toothpick.

Spray the lower rack with nonstick cooking spray. Place the stuffed filets on the rack. Lay 1 lem slice on each filet. Squeeze the juice from 1 lemon over the fillets.
Cook at 350° for 20 minutes.

Salmon with Dill and a Butter-Maple Glaze

PREP TIME: 10 minutes   COOK TIME: 20 minutes   SERVES: 4-6

We wholeheartedly recommend that if you buy salmon, buy wild-caught Alaskan or Scottish salmon instead of farm-raised. It is a healthier, leaner product, and besides, it's just environmental good sense. Farmed salmon consume more fish than they generate as a final product. As salmon farms have grown, many forage fish are being over-harvested and turned into fish food for salmon. This just cannot be sustained. Do the world a favor...stick with wild-caught.

1 large Salmon fillet (about 8" by 5", heart of the fillet)
4 TBS Butter, melted
¼ cup Maple Syrup
1 TBS fresh Dill

Combine the melted butter and the maple syrup in a bowl and mix well.

Coat the salmon fillet well with the glaze mixture, then sprinkle over with the dill.

Place the salmon on the upper rack in the oven. Cook at 325° for 20 minutes or until the fish is easily flaked with the tines of a fork.

Thai Crab Imperial

PREP: 3 minutes   COOK: 10 minutes   SERVES: 4

The key to success with crab is the quality of your ingredients. We recommend you get the freshest crab you can, just picked being preferred. If you are going to pay good money for the crab, you may as well take the time to make the aioli and the garlic chili sauce from scratch. It makes all the difference and doesn't take any longer than finding a store that carries them. Crab imperial also makes a great stuffing for fish or shrimp and can be baked on top of hot pretzels for a super special treat.

½ cup Breadcrumbs, unseasoned
1 Egg, beaten
½ cup Mayo or Aioli Sauce
2 TBS Milk
3 TBS Thai Sweet Garlic Chili Sauce (page 116)
1 pound crab, fresh, cleaned and flaked
4 TBS Parmesan, grated
2 TBS Butter

Mix breadcrumbs, egg, milk, chili sauce and crab together and place in small, oven-safe ramekins. Top with Parmesan and dot with Butter.

Bake on the lower rack of the SuperWave Oven for 10 minutes at 350º. This is wonderful as a main course or if served with Crusty Garlic Bread (page 47).

Aioli Sauce

PREP: 10 minutes   MAKES: 2 ½ cups

4 Egg Yolks
2 cups Olive Oil
12 cloves Garlic, peeled
2 tsp Dijon Mustard
1 tsp Black Pepper
2 TBS Fresh Lemon Juice
Dash Hot Sauce

Combine egg yolks, garlic, mustard, pepper, lemon juice and hot sauce in a food processor and blend until smooth. With the machine running, add olive oil in a thin stream until it is all incorporated and you have a smooth, thick mayonnaise.

Lobster Medallions
with Shrimp and Scallops in a Garlic-Lemon Butter

PREP TIME: 10-15 minutes   COOK TIME: 15 minutes   SERVES: 4

Shakespeare might have proposed music as the food of love, but personally, we'd pick lobster. And what could make lobster any better? How about scallops and shrimp? Serve this one to someone you adore, but be ready for the repercussions! Feel the love, baby.

2	medium to large Lobster tails, very cold but not frozen
12	large Shrimp, peeled and deveined, rinsed and pat dried
1	cup medium-sized Dry Pack Scallops, rinsed and pat dried
4-6	TBS Butter, melted
4	cloves Garlic, finely minced
3	TBS Shallot, finely minced
	Juice of one lemon
2	cups Sugar Snap Peas, washed and strings removed
1	Red Bell Pepper, seeded and sliced into ½" long strips
	pinch of Salt, twist of Pepper

Pull the lobster tail from its shell, and slicing across the tail, cut them into several medallions, approximately ½" thick.

In a large glass bowl, combine the melted butter, minced garlic, minced shallot, and the lemon juice. Stir to blend well. Add the lobster, shrimps and scallops to the bowl, toss to coat well, and let sit in the fridge for about a half an hour.

When ready to cook, place the Sugar Snap Peas and the Pepper strips on the bottom rack of the SuperWave. Sprinkle with the salt and pepper. Place the lobster, shrimp and scallops on the top rack above the vegetables, making sure to place them so they won't fall through the tines of the rack.

Cook at 350° for 15 minutes or until the shellfish is opaque, white, and firm, and the vegetables are crisp-tender. Serve with the Garlic-Butter sauce on the side to add as desired.

Salmon Rounds
with Horseradish-Dill Stuffing

PREP: 15 minutes   COOK: 8-10 minutes   SERVES: 2 entrée. 4-6 appetizer

This recipe comes to us via a grand friend of our parents. Dear old Mac was a little banty rooster of a man, 5 foot 3 inches tall on his tippy toes and all of 95 pounds sopping wet. We never saw Mac without a chewed-up cigar stub in his mouth, a porkpie hat on his head, or a rolled up race form in his jacket pocket, but, oh, that man could cook! He spent most of his free time fishing or crabbing and knew just what to do with anything that lived in water. Here is our version of one of Mac's favorites.

½ cup finely crumbled fresh Breadcrumbs
1 TBS minced yellow Onion
¼ cup minced Dill Pickle Gherkins
¾ TBS minced fresh Sage
1 tsp minced fresh Thyme
Salt and freshly ground Pepper to taste
2½ TBS unsalted Butter, melted
¼ to 1/3 cup prepared Horseradish
¼ cup light Cream or Milk
**   Dill Pickle juice**
1 1-pound Salmon fillet (about ¾" thick
**   at center, skin removed, sliced**
**   horizontally to ¼" thickness)**

Prepare the stuffing by combining the breadcrumbs, onion, pickle, and herbs in a bowl. Season to taste with salt and pepper. Mix thoroughly, then add the butter, horseradish, cream, and enough of the dill pickle juice to achieve a moist (though not "wet") stuffing mixture. Set aside.

Lay the salmon pieces flat on your work surface. Season with a little salt and pepper. Carefully place a layer of the stuffing mixture across the entire surface of the fillet pieces. It should be between 1/16 and 1/8 inch thick. Then roll up each piece jelly roll style, and secure by tying at either end with light, wet, cotton string.

Place the rolls on the tall rack of the SuperWave and bake at 375º for 8-10 minutes. Remove from the oven, discard the string. Let cool slightly, then carefully slice medallions ½" thick and arrange them on a plate. Top with a dollup of horseradish, if desired.

Super Seafood Cakes

PREP: 12 minutes   COOK: 12 minutes   SERVES: 4

We threw these little gems together one summer night down at the Delaware shore. We had come to the end of our seaside vacation and had a selection of seafood left uneaten, but with not any one item in quantity enough to feed everyone the same thing. So we mixed them all together and this is what we came up with. Serve these with a little slaw or salad for a very happy crew.

3 Eggs, beaten
4 TBS Mayonnaise or Aioli (page 81)
½ tsp cracked Black Pepper
1 ¼ tsp dry Mustard
¼ tsp Cayenne Pepper
1 tsp Parsley Flakes
½ tsp Tarragon
½ pound Backfin Crab Meat, picked and flaked
½ pound fresh Salmon, skinned and minced
½ pound minced Clams
1/2 can smoked Oysters
1 cup Saltine Crackers, crushed fine
2 tsp Lemon Juice
Breadcrumbs for coating

Mash the oysters and clams together, then add in the Salmon and crab and mix thoroughly. Set aside.

Beat the mayonnaise into the eggs, add the peppers, mustard and herbs and mix. Add to the seafood mixture and blend, then add the crackers and lemon juice and mix again until homogenous.

Form into 8 cakes. Combine the two racks (put the short on top of the tall) and place of the cakes on the racks in the SuperWave Oven. Bake at 375º for about 6 minutes. Remove the short rack with the 4 cakes and place it in the bottom of the SuperWave. Put the remaining 4 cakes on the top rack. Bake again at 350º for another 12 minutes. All 8 cakes should now be ready to serve.

Casserdies

Chicken and Rice Casserole

PREP: 30 minutes   COOK: 30 minutes   MAKES: one 8" or 10" casserole

This was one of the first dishes we learned to cook, start to finish, on our own. Mom had been watching Julia Child on PBS and decided her young men should know how to make at least one foolproof meal. We'd never starve that way, you see. Apparently Julia had been making somethin similar to this on her show that day, so this is what Mom chose to have us do. Lucky for us, it was a great choice and we still make and enjoy it to this day. Thanks Mom.

1 cup Celery, finely chopped
1 small Onion, chopped
1 small Green Pepper, chopped
2 TBS Butter
2 sprigs Parsley, minced
½ cup Flour
1 cup Milk
2 cups Chicken Broth
   Salt and Pepper to taste
1½ cups Rice, cooked and then rinsed well
4 cups cooked Chicken (light and dark meats) cut into chunks
2 cups grated Cheddar or Swiss Cheese
1 ½ cups crushed Corn Flakes
3 TBS melted Butter

In a skillet over medium-high heat, brown the celery, onion, pepper, and parsley in the butter. Blend in the flour milk, and chicken broth, and stir well t blend. Season to taste with the salt and pepper. Simmer over low heat until a smooth gravy forms.

Butter a shallow 8" or 10" baking dish Cover the bottom with half the rice, then ladle over with a layer of half the gravy. Add a layer of half the chicken, then a layer of half the cheese. Repeat the layers again.

Mix the crushed corn flakes with the melted butter and sprinkle on top.

Bake on the lower rack of the SuperWave at 300° for about 30 minutes.

Boatman's Stew

PREP: 4 minutes   COOK: 25 minutes   SERVES: 4

Imagine yourself sitting on a dock in Key West, watching the sun set in the West. A small trawler, looking more barnacle than boat, chugs up and ties off right next to you. The skipper says hello, introduces you to his wife and his six toed cat, and invites you to share a drink. Before it's all over, you have a full belly, new friends and this recipe tucked into your pocket. Now you know how we learned how to make this dish. Enjoy.

2 lbs. firm White Fish, cut in 2 inch squares
1 TBS flour
4 Green Onions, chopped
2 TBS Olive Oil
¼ tsp red pepper
½ tsp Black Pepper, course grind
1 cup Half and Half
2/3 cup White Wine
1 tsp Tarragon, dried or fresh
1 clove Garlic, minced
3 TBS fresh Italian Parsley, chopped

Dredge the fish squares in the flour just to coat.

Whisk together the Half and Half, olive oil, wine, red and black pepper, tarragon, green onion and parsley. Add the fish chunks and pour all into an 8" casserole.

Place on the lower rack of the SuperWave Oven and simmer for 25 minutes at 375°. Stir once after about 12 minutes, then continue simmering.

Serve with warmed Italian bread.

Shepherd's Pie

PREP: 20 minutes   COOK: 15 minutes   SERVES: 6

In doing our research for this recipe we found out there are no less than twenty different names for this same dish worldwide. We suppose that makes shepherd's pie the world's universal comfort food. This version has been around since the 18th Century and it's every bit as good today as it was for our founding fathers.

2 cups lean ground Beef, Lamb or Turkey
½ cup Onion, chopped
1 tsp Olive Oil
1 clove Garlic, minced
½ tsp Salt
¼ tsp Pepper
2 cups Frozen Vegetables of your choice
1 jar Gravy
3 Potatoes, boiled, drained and mashed
4 oz Cheddar Cheese, grated

In a large skillet over medium-high heat, brown the meat with onion, garlic and oil.
Remove from heat and mix in a large bowl with the vegetables, gravy, salt, pepper, and cheese.

Pour into a shallow 8" or 10" casserole. Top with the mashed potatoes, spread evenly over the top. Bake on lower rack in SuperWave for 15 minutes at 375°.

Scalloped Potatoes with Ground Beef

PREP: 20 minutes   COOK: About 25 minutes   MAKES: one 10" casserole

Casseroles are comfort food that everyone in the family loves. We challenge you to find a more comfortable dish than this. It's a classic. One dish. Meat and potatoes. Yum.

½ pound Ground Beef
1 Onion, finely chopped
1 TBS Olive Oil
2 cups Potatoes, sliced into 1/8" thick rounds
**   Salt and Pepper to taste**
1 cup Milk
2 TBS Sour Cream

Brown the beef and onion quickly in the olive oil.

In a shallow 10" casserole, place a thin layer of the potatoes, then a layer of the beef and onion mixture. Repeat layers until all beef and potatoes are used. Do not pack it tightly. Season with salt and pepper to taste.

Blend the milk and sour cream and pour over the casserole just enough to fill ¾ of the depth of the ingredients. Place on lower rack and bake slowly at 325° for about 25 minutes or until warmed through and bubbly.

Variations: This casserole allows for any number of added ingredients…chopped celery, green peas, green or red peppers, and/or cheese. You can also "heat it up" with the addition of some jalapeno or hot peppers, if desired.

Tuna Fish Casserole

PREP: 30 minutes   COOK: 12 minutes   MAKES: one 8" casserole

Mom was a painter of landscapes, still lifes and poodle skirts. Her talent was widely noted in our little town and she commanded a decent sum for the custom work she did. She was notorious in our house, however, for getting caught up in the creative "zone" and suddenly realizing it was half an hour to dinner time. She always had a few of these quick recipes up her sleeve just in case. This is a dandy.

2 cups Bechamel (White) Sauce
   Salt and Pepper to taste
1 can chunk light or albacore Tuna
1 can Condensed Cream of Mushroom Soup
1 can Water
1 cup Green Peas
1 cup grated American Cheese
   Potato chips

Prepare the white sauce in a small saucepan. Season with salt and pepper to taste. Add the mushroom soup and the water, stirring well. Simmer over low heat. Add the peas and tuna, mixing well. Layer the bottom of a greased 8" casserole with the potato chips, then cover with half the sauce mixture. Do another layer of potato chips, then top that with the rest of the sauce mixture. Sprinkle across the top with the cheese.

Bake on the lower rack of the SuperWave at 350° for about 12 minutes.

Bechamel Sauce

PREP: 10 minutes   COOK: 20-25 minutes   MAKES: about 3 cups

5 TBS Butter
¼ cup flour
1 quart Milk
2 tsp Salt
¼ tsp ground Nutmeg

In a small saucepan, melt the butter, then slowly mix in the flour, stirring constantly with a fork until well blended. Cook over low heat until the roux is lightly browned. Add the milk slowly, a little at a time, until the milk has been thickened by the roux. Simmer until the flour is softened and no longer gritty, about 20-25 minutes. If sauce thickens too much in that time, add a little more milk. The consistency should end up being like good, thick gravy.

Asian Cashew Chicken Casserole

PREP: 30 minutes   COOK: 25 minutes   SERVES: 6

Our sister, Maggie, is a genius with a casserole. She can take a counter full of unrelated random ingredients, put them together in a single dish and make you believe she had always had that in th[e] master plan. She just has a way with the balance and interplay of flavors, and she loves puzzles.

This is one dish she puzzled out rather than ordering in Chinese. Try adding drop or two of sesame oil for a delicio[us] variation. Just great!

1 to 2 TBS extra virgin Olive Oil
2 pounds boneless, skinless Chicken
**   (white and dark) cut into 1" chunks**
1 cup finely chopped Celery
¼ cup finely chopped Yellow Onion
1 cup grated Carrot
½ cup finely chopped Green Pepper
1 TBS chopped fresh Tarragon
salt and freshly ground Pepper to taste
1 11-oz can Mushroom Soup (undiluted)
½ cup Chicken Broth
1 5-oz can of Chinese Noodles
1 cup whole and broken Cashews

In a large skillet over medium-high heat, heat the olive oil, then add the chicken chunks and cook until browne[d] slightly. Using a slotted spoon, remov[e] the chicken from the pan and place in [a] large bowl.

Add the celery, onion, carrot, green pepper, and tarragon and gently toss to mix well. Season with the salt and pepper to taste.

In a medium bowl, mix together the mushroom soup and the chicken broth.

In a shallow 10" casserole dish, place a layer of the Chinese noodles. Add half the chicken mixtur[e] then pour half the soup and broth mix evenly over the top. Top this with another layer of the noodles, the rest of the chicken mixture and the rest of the soup and broth mix. Top with the cashews.

Place the casserole on the bottom rack of the SuperWave and bake at 350° for about 25 minutes, [or] until the casserole is cooked through.

Lima Bean Mini-Casseroles

PREP: 20 minutes   COOK: 10-12 Minutes   MAKES: 4-6 small casseroles

Lima beans are amazing. They have been in cultivation as long as corn in the Americas, the earliest archeological specimens dating from 2000 BC from the Andes to Mexico. They are a virtually fat free source of high-quality protein and studies show they may prevent heart disease and provide slow-burning energy that balances blood sugar levels. This isn't just great food, it's preventive medicine

½ medium Onion, chopped
½ pound of Sausage meat
2 cups Tomato Sauce
½ tsp Poultry Seasoning
1 TBS Brown Sugar
1 tsp Salt
½ cup of the liquor from the beans
¼ cup Breadcrumbs
1 16-oz can of whole Lima Beans, liquid
    drained off but reserved
¼ cup shredded Cheddar Cheese

Brown the onion in a skillet with the sausage, stirring to break up the sausage to smaller bits. Add all other ingredients but the lima beans and cheese.
Divide the limas equally among 4-6 small round casseroles or ramekins, depending upon their size. Cover the beans in each mini-casserole with equal amounts of the sausage mixture. Top with equal amounts of the cheese.

Bake on the upper rack of the SuperWave at 350° for 10-12 minutes.

Homemade Poultry Seasoning

1 tsp ground Sage
1½ tsp ground Thyme
1 tsp ground Marjoram
3/4 tsp ground Rosemary
1/2 tsp Nutmeg
1/2 tsp finely ground Black Pepper

Mix all ingredients thoroughly in mortar. Grind until soft and fine. Store in a tightly closed spice bottle.

Kedgeree

PREP: 10 minutes   COOK: 15 minutes   SERVES: 6-8

This is a centuries old dish believed to be brought back to Britain by the colonials who had enjoyed it in India. For them, it was considered a breakfast dish and filled the spot Americans had for hash. It certainly makes a hearty breakfast, but does quite nicely on the dinner table as well.

6 TBS Butter
1 TBS Curry Powder
3 cups Rice, cooked
2 pound White Fish, chopped into small chunks
1 tsp Salt
4 Hard Boiled Eggs, finely chopped
Juice of ½ Lemon
½ cup Parsley, chopped
   Dash Worcestershire Sauce
¼ cup Milk

In a large bowl, mix all the ingredients and pour into a shallow casserole dish. Bake on the lower rack in the SuperWave for 15 minutes at 350º.

Chicken and Corn Pudding

PREP: 5 minutes   COOK: 25 minutes   SERVES:

There are all manner of corn pudding recipes out there, but we like this the best because it is so simple, so fast and so tasty.

2 cups canned or cooked Chicken, diced
3 Eggs, beaten
3 cups Milk
2 TBS Flour
1 ½ tsp Salt
1/8 tsp Black Pepper, coarsely ground
¼ cup Onion, chopped
½ tsp Thyme
½ tsp Rosemary
¼ cup Green Pepper, chopped
2 cups Corn

Grease a shallow 8" or 10" casserole dish and place the diced chicken in a layer across the bottom. Mix together all other ingredients and pour over the chicken.
Bake on the lower rack of the SuperWave for 25 minutes at 325º.

Spinach Rockefeller

PREP: 10 minutes   COOK: 12 minutes   SERVES: 6

For those of you looking to cook lighter and with an eye to better nutrition and health, this is the recipe for you. We could eat this for any meal of the day, but it doubles nicely as a side dish if necessary. For the family Christmas Eve gatherings one of us usually comes through with the oystered version, but either way, this dish is good for what ails you.

2 Eggs, separated
2 Pkgs (20 oz) frozen chopped Spinach, thawed and drained
½ cup Butter
¾ cup Breadcrumbs
¼ cup Onion, grated
1/8 tsp Thyme
½ tsp Garlic Powder
2 dashes Tabasco
½ tsp Salt
¼ tsp Black Pepper
¼ cup Parmesan, grated

In a bowl, beat the egg yolks until light yellow, then gently mix in the spinach. In a separate bowl, combine the butter, breadcrumbs, onion, thyme, garlic powder, Tabasco, salt, pepper, and parmesan. Add this into the spinach mixture. Beat the egg whites until stiff and gently fold into the spinach mixture. Pour this into a shallow 10" casserole dish and place on the low rack of the SuperWave. Bake at 350° for 12 minutes.

Variation: *For a holiday treat, line the bottom of the casserole dish with plump oysters and bake as directed. Delicious!*

Salmon Tomato Casserole

PREP: 10 minutes   COOK: 8-10 minutes   SERVES: 4-6

We have friends, the Beagles, who for years ran a truck stand selling vegetables grown on their family farm. As the next generation came along, it became obvious that the pups weren't intereste in continuing with it, but our friends never figured out how to grow less produce. So now, every year, we end up with bushels of homegrown tomatoes we must figure o what to do with. This dish is one fine way and comes highly recommended b Don Beagle himself.

- **2 cups cooked Salmon**
  (smoked Salmon will work well too)
- **1 ½ cups cooked Tomatoes**
  (a 14-16 oz can of tomatoes is fine)
- **1 TBS melted Butter**
- **1 ¾ cup Bread or Cracker Crumbs**
- **1 Egg, well beaten**
- **1 TBS Tarragon**

Flake the salmon…remove all bones i any there. Combine all ingredients in a bowl, and mix lightly with two forks – don't break up any larger chunks of salmon if you can hel it.

Pour into a shallow, greased 10" casserole dish. Place on lower rack of SuperWave and bake at 425° for about 8-10 minutes.

Pumpkin Pancetta Penne

PREP: 5 minutes   COOK: 20 minutes   SERVES: 4

There are few flavors as delicious in tandem as garlic and bacon. They make just about anything taste great. As proof of that, this recipe comes to us from young David Tomasacci, a doctoral candidate and gourmand at Ohio State University who came up with a way to feed himself each fall by converting uncut Halloween pumpkins into college cuisine. This recipe is fabulous, and not just because it has garlic and bacon, although that doesn't hurt.

4 oz Pancetta or Prociutto, or 4 strips Bacon
2 cloves Garlic, minced
1 medium Onion, chopped fine
2 cups (1 pound) Pumpkin, pureed or canned
½ cup White Wine
1 TBS fresh Tarragon, minced
5 TBS fresh Parsley, minced
½ cup fresh Parmesan, grated
Pinch Cinnamon
Pinch Nutmeg
Toasted Pumpkin Seeds for garnish
8 oz Penne

Place the pancetta/bacon/prosciutto, onion and garlic in in a shallow 8" or 10" cake pan on the top rack of the SuperWave and cook off at 400° until bacon is just crisp (about 4 minutes). Drain and chop.

Place this mixture in a large saucepan. Whisk in the pumpkin, wine, parsley, cinnamon, nutmeg and tarragon. Heat through and set aside.

Cook off the penne until slightly underdone (about 8 minutes). Drain, then toss with pumpkin mixture until thoroughly coated.

Place in a shallow 10" casserole dish. Top with the parmesan cheese and place on the lower rack in the SuperWave to bake for 10 minutes at 375°.

Garnish with Toasted Pumpkin Seeds and serve.

Variations: Try this dish with a Spinach Tagliatelle or Spinach Linguini for a beautiful and delicious change of pace.

Meatless Main Dishes

Garden Lasagne

PREP: 1 hour (sauce). 15 minutes (pasta)   COOK: 25 minutes   SERVES: 6

Vegetarian fare need not be boring, and this dish proves it. The variety of chunky vegetables in the sauce, along with the layers of noodles and spinach make for a luscious meal. Try thinly sliced Portobello mushrooms on top of each layer of spinach for a variation with nice dense texture.

SAUCE
¾ cup sliced Mushrooms
½ cup chopped Celery
¼ cup chopped Green Pepper
¼ cup chopped Onion
1 Garlic clove, minced
1½ TBS Olive Oil
½ 12-oz. can Italian Plum Tomatoes
½ 8-oz can Tomato Sauce
½ 6-oz can Tomato Paste
1 TBS fresh Parsley, minced
salt and feshly ground Pepper to taste
¾ cup Water
1 cup Zucchini, sliced thin

LASAGNE
6 ounces Lasagna Noodles
½ pound Ricotta cheese
1 Egg (optional)
5 ounces chopped fresh Spinach
¾ cup shredded Mozzarella or Provolone Cheese
¼ to ½ cup grated Parmesan cheese

For Sauce: Saute the mushrooms, celery, green pepper, onion, and garlic in the oil for about 5 minutes in a large stockpot. Add the tomatoes, the tomato sauce, tomato paste, seasonings, and ½ of the water. Simmer, covered, for about 1 hour. Add the remaining water and simmer 15 minutes longer. When the sauce is finished simmering, add the zucchini.

For Lasagne:
Cook the noodles in boiling, salted water. While cooking, mix together the ricotta, egg, and spinach.

Squash Boats

PREP: 25 minutes   COOK: 8 minutes   SERVES: 4 Main Course/8 Side Dish

Squash are nature's bread bowls. They can be used to hold chili, soups, sweet glazes of all sorts, or in this case, vegetable stuffing. While these make a marvelous main course, they are also delicious side dishes for any other entree you might like to serve.

½ cup chopped Onion
½ cup chopped Celery
1 Garlic clove, crushed
2 TBS vegetable oil
1 cup chopped, peeled Tomatoes
1 cup sliced fresh Mushrooms
¾ cup cooked White Rice
2 TBS chopped fresh flat leaf Parsley
1 TBS chopped fresh Basil
1 tsp Salt
½ tsp freshly ground Pepper
3-4 yellow Squash or green Zucchini,
   or some of both
½ cup grated Parmesan Cheese

In a large skillet over medium-high heat, sauté the onion, celery, and garlic in the oil until golden. Remove to a bowl, and stir in the tomatoes and mushrooms, the rice and seasonings, and cook just until hot. Add back the onion mixture and combine. Meanwhile, cut the squash in half lengthwise, and blanch in salted, boiling water for 3-4 minutes. Remove carefully and set on a flat work surface. Using a teaspoon or melon baller, scrape out the seeds and pulp. Leave about 1/8 inch walls. Place the stuffing into the squash shells. Don't overpack them so the stuffing is hard and tight. Mound it a little, as it will settle slightly when baking.

Place the shells on the racks of the oven and bake at 350° for about 7-8 minutes. For the last 2 minutes, top them with the Parmesan cheese, so it melts into the stuffing a little.

Tip: For these boats, set them into the grooves of the rack, so they remain upright while cooking and don't roll over. You might also try topping them with a little tomato sauce, if desired.

Variation: If you'd like to add some ground turkey or beef to these, it's not a problem. Just mix in about a pound of either at the point when you're adding in the tomatoes, mushrooms, rice and seasonings.

Ultimate Veggie Burgers

PREP: 15 minutes   COOK: 11 minutes   MAKES: 8 burgers

A friend of ours recently found out he has a medical condition that, once treated, can likely be held in remission with proper diet. One of the things he must avoid is meat, especially grilled meat. Being a burger lover, that was a blow to our friend until we introduced him to this healthy alternative. When meatless is this tasty, who needs meat?

1 medium Onion, chopped medium fine
2 Carrots, peeled and shredded
1 Rutabaga or Turnip, peeled and grated
1 Yellow Squash, grated
1 small Beet, grated
2 cloves Garlic
1 tsp Cumin, ground
½ tsp Coriander, ground
2 TBS Olive Oil
½ cup Breadcrumbs, seasoned
1½ cups Mashed Potatoes
½ cup Rice, cooked
1 TBS fresh Basil, minced
Pinch Salt and Pepper
  Corn Meal

In a bowl, toss the onion, carrot, rutabaga, squash, beet, garlic, coriander and cumin with olive oil coat. Put the mixture in a baking di and place on the tall rack of the Superwave Oven and cook at 375º for 5 minutes. Vegetables should b soft but not browned.
Remove the vegetables from the oven and place again in the bowl.

Mix in the breadcrumbs, potatoes, rice, basil, salt and pepper until smooth.
Using ¾ cup of mix for each, make patties and dust lightly with corn meal.

Place on the top rack in the Superwave at 425º for 3 minutes per side or until slightly brown.

Wild Mushroom, Apple and Olive Empanadas

PREP: 20 minutes   COOK: 6-8 minutes   MAKES: one 10" pie

Empanadas are a hidden treasure presentation hailing from Spain. You can make them any size but a size where two or three of them make up a serving is ideal. The keys to this recipe are the mushrooms you use. A variety produces a much more interesting flavor profile than a single mushroom type. If you can get your hands on some fresh morels, add them sparingly to the filling for a real treat.

DOUGH:
- 3 cups All-Purpose Flour
- 1 tsp Salt
- 4 TBS cold Butter, cut into small pieces
- ½ cup Ice Water

FILLING:
- 12 ounces Wild Mushrooms, half of which are finely minced, the other half sliced thinly (a blend of shiitake, enoki and oyster are best)
- 1 medium Red Onion, chopped fine
- 1 Red Bell Pepper, chopped fine
- 1 Red Delicious Apple, chopped fine
- ¾ cup Black Olives, pitted and minced
- 2 TBS Olive Oil
- 2 Roma Tomatoes, chopped fine
- 1 tsp Thyme, dried
- 2 TBS Parsley, minced
- 1 TBS Tarragon, dried
- 2 cloves Garlic, minced
- ¼ cup White Wine
- ½ tsp Salt
- ¼ tsp Black Pepper, coarsely ground

In a medium bowl, sift together the flour and salt. Cut in the butter until the mixture forms small crumbs. Mix in the ice water 1 TBS at a time until a stiff dough forms. Cover and allow to rest while you prepare the filling.

In an oven safe dish, place mushrooms, onion, peppers, apple, olive oil and tomatoes. Broil on the top rack of the Superwave Oven at 450° for 5 minutes, until the mushrooms and tomatoes give up their liquid.

Remove the pan from oven and pour off the liquid, placing it in a saucepan along with the herbs and garlic. Add the wine, olives, salt and pepper and reduce over medium heat until the mixture is thickening into a glaze.

Stir the mushroom mixture into wine glaze and add the breadcrumbs. Stir to blend.

Roll out the dough on a floured surface until 1/8" thick. Cut into 5" circles. Spoon about 2 tablespoons of the mushroom mixture into each of the dough rounds and seal the edges by crimping with the tines of a fork.

Bake the empanadas on the racks of the Superwave at 375° for 7 minutes or until golden brown.

Vegetarian Pizza

PREP: 20 minutes   COOK: 6-8 minutes   MAKES one 10" pie

When asked what food they would find served in heaven, kindergarten children overwhelmingly name pizza as the most likely candidate for a nosh in the hereafter. This recipe surely proves that pizza can be heavenly here on earth as well.

8-10 cloves Garlic, peeled
2 TBS Olive Oil
1 medium Red Onion, cut into rings about ¼" thick
1/3 cup oil-packed Sun-dried Tomatoes, drained, oil reserved
1 10" frozen Pizza Crust
1½ cups grated Mozzarella cheese
½ cup roasted Red Peppers (jar type), cut into ½-inch-thick strips
½ cup crumbled Feta cheese
3 TBS chopped fresh Basil
1 TBS chopped fresh Parsley

Place the small rack atop the small rack to form a grid. Place the garlic cloves and the onion rings on the racks. Bake at 375° for 10 minutes. Remove and cool.

When the garlic cloves are cooled, place them in a food processor and add the sun-dried tomatoes and pulse until a smooth paste forms. If you need to, add a teaspoon of olive oil at a time until a smooth, spreadable paste is created. Spread the garlic/tomato paste over the pizza crust. Top with the mozzarella cheese, the baked onions, the peppers, and the feta. Sprinkle with half of the basil and half of the parsley.

Bake on the top rack of the SuperWave at 450° for 6-7 minutes or until the crust is golden brown and the cheese is bubbly. Remove from the oven and let cool a couple of minutes, then top with the remaining basil and parsley. Cut and serve.

Zucchini Pie

PREP: 25 minutes   COOK: 20 minutes   SERVES: 6-7

We always grew zucchini in our family garden. Invariably, each season Dad would miss one or two of them when they were small and a week or two later would pull out enormous ten pound squash he called "war clubs". Most of the time we would make zucchini relish out of them, but every now and then Mom would treat us with this zucchini pie. We loved every bite. So will you.

4 cups thinly sliced Zucchini
1 cup Onion, chopped
½ cup unsalted Butter or Margarine
½ cup chopped fresh Parsley
½ tsp Salt
½ tsp freshly ground Pepper
¼ tsp Garlic Powder
¼ tsp chopped fresh Basil
¼ tsp chopped fresh Oregano
2 Eggs, beaten
2 cups shredded Mozzarella cheese
1 TBS Dijon mustard
1 8-10" Pie Crust

In a large skillet, sauté the zucchini and onion the butter until the zucchini is softened and the onions are translucent, about 5 minutes. Stir in the chopped parsley, salt, pepper, garlic powde basil, and oregano.

In a large mixing bowl, combine the eggs, cheese, and mustard, then add the zucchini/oni mixure and stir together. Pour this mixure into the pie crust and place the pie on the lower rack of the SuperWave. Bake at 375º for 15 minutes o until the crust is nicely browned and the zucchini/cheese center is melted and bubbly. Remove from the oven and let stand 10 minutes before serving.

Superwave Samosas

PREP: 13 minutes   COOK: 7 minutes   Makes: 4 large samosas

Samosas are sold in one form or another all across eastern and central Asia, usually by street vendors who each have their own unique recipe for the dish. In Nepal, they call them Momos (moe-moes) and are a daily part of the Nepalese diet. This recipe is a variation on an original Momo recipe brought home by a doctor friend whose wife learned how to make them while he was on duty for Doctors Without Borders in Katmandu. We can see why the Nepalese eat these every day!

3 TBS Olive Oil
   Dash Tabasco
1 tsp Coriander Seeds
¼ cup Shallots, minced
1 tsp Ginger, freshly grated
2 clove Garlic, crushed
1¼ pounds Potatoes, boiled until tender,
   cooled, peeled and cut into ½ inch cubes
1 TBS Curry Powder
¼ tsp Black Pepper, coarsely ground
   Pinch each Cinnamon, Nutmeg,
Cardamom, Clove
½ cup frozen Green Peas, thawed
2 tsp fresh Lemon Juice
2 tsp Soy Sauce
½ tsp Salt
1 batch Naan Bread dough

Heat the oil in a large skillet over medium-high heat. Add the coriander seeds and cook until they darken slightly. Add the shallots, ginger, and garlic and cook about 2 minutes. Add the diced potatoes, curry, pepper, and the pinches of spice to the skillet and sauté about 3 more minutes. Remove from heat and add the peas, lemon juice, soy sauce, and salt mixing gently. Let the filling cool completely.

Divide the batch of Naan Bread dough into 8 portions, and roll out to 1/8" thick on a floured surface. Fill liberally with the Samosa filling, then fold over and pinch edges with the tines of a fork to seal. Bake on the top rack of the Superwave at 325º until golden brown. Drizzle with Spicy Cilantro Dip.

Spicy Cilantro Dip

PREP: 10 minutes   MAKES: 2 cups sauce

You'll love this no matter what you put it on!

1 cup fresh Cilantro, packed
½ cup fresh Lemon Juice
¼ cup Walnuts, chopped
1 Serrano Pepper, stemmed and seeded
1 large clove Garlic, crushed
1 TSB Lawry's Season Salt
2 TBS Hot Oil
2 TBS Sugar
  Salt to taste

Combine all the ingredients except the salt in a food processor and purée thoroughly. Transfer to a bowl and add salt to taste.

Naan Bread

PREP: 35 minutes (not counting rising)   COOK: 5 minutes   MAKES: 4 breads

We are offering this as a base for samosas, but if you bake these as a larger round, they make wonderful sides for curries or other saucy dishes.

1 tsp Dried Yeast
1 tsp Sugar or Honey
  warm water
2 cup Flour
 ¼ tsp Salt
½ tsp Baking Powder
2 TBS Plain Yogurt
2 TBS Whole Milk
1 TBS Olive Oil
1 tsp Rosemary, ground
1 TBS Curry Powder

Mix the yeast with the sugar or honey and 2 TBS warm water. Set aside until frothy. In a mixing bowl, blend the flour, rosemary, salt, and baking powder. Add in yogurt, milk, yeast mixture, and the olive oil.
Mix together well, then knead in the bowl until soft and slightly springy. Cover and allow to rise for 30 minutes.
Punch down the dough, then divide into 4 portions and roll each portion out into a round ¼" thick.

Carefully place the rounds on the racks of the SuperWave and bake in the at 275° for 5 minutes or until bread is lightly golden brown. Bake in 2 batches, if necessary.

Easy Lentil Loaf

PREP: 10 minutes   COOK: 25 minutes   SERVES: 4

This is a great dish that is more than merely vegetarian. It is a vegan delight delivering whole protein without eggs, dairy or animal products of any kind. The key is to avoid pressing the mix too firmly into the pan. Use a light touch and you will end up with a better loaf. If you are lucky enough to have any leftovers, try frying up a slice in some olive oil for breakfast. It's delicious!

2 cup Lentils, cooked
1 cup Brown Rice, cooked
½ cup Red Bell Pepper, chopped
½ cup Onion, chopped
½ cup Roma Tomato, chopped
¼ cup Celery, chopped
½ cup Bread Crumbs, seasoned
3 TBS fresh Parsley, chopped
2 tsp fresh Basil, minced
1 tsp dried Oregano
½ tsp dried Marjoram
¼ tsp Black Pepper
2 tsp Water
1 recipe Thai Sweet Garlic Chili Sauce

Combine all the ingredients in a large bowl and press lightly into a non-stick 10" loaf pan.
Set the pan on the low rack and bake in the Superwave at 350º for 25 minutes.
Top with Thai Sweet Garlic Chili Sauce for the last 5 minutes.

Thai Sweet Garlic Chile Sauce

PREP: 8 minutes   COOK: 10 minutes   MAKES: 1 ½ cups

2 Hot Chilies of your choice, minced (Habanero for very hot, cayenne for less hot)
1 cup Maple Syrup
1 ½ TBS Rice Vinegar
2 TBS Dry Sherry
2 TBS Soy Sauce
1 tsp fresh Ginger, minced
2 cloves Garlic, crushed
1/8 tsp Black Pepper

Mix together all ingredients.
Place in oven safe dish on the bottom rack of the SuperWave Oven.

Cook at 350º and stir every 3 minutes for a total of 10 minutes or until thickened.

Sides

Crusty Parmesan Potato Wedges

PREP TIME: 5 minutes   COOK TIME: 20 minutes   SERVES: 4

"Boo-yaw!" is an expression used in sports when an athlete makes a particularly spectacular play. Some side dishes are subtle, some are more assertive, but this one stands up and screams "Boo-yaw!" Serve them with big flavored entrees like barbecue, steak or dense meaty fish like tuna or swordfish. Now, that's a spectacular play! Boo-yaw!

½ cup Olive Oil
1 TBS Garlic Herb seasoning
½ tsp Pepper
½ tsp Salt
½ tsp Paprika
1 tsp Oregano
¼ cup Parmesan Cheese
2 large Potatoes, cut into wedges

In a bowl, mix together the olive oil, garlic herb seasoning, pepper, salt, paprika, oregano and Parmesan cheese. Add in the potato wedges and toss to coat well. Spray the upper rack of the SuperWave with nonstick cooking spray. Place the potato wedges on the rack. Cook at 350° for 20 minutes or until well-browned and crispy.

Mushroom Turnovers

PREP: 30 minutes (excluding dough)   COOK: 10 minutes   MAKES: 12 turnovers

Genetic biologists along with archeologists have evidence that mushrooms showed up on this planet around the same time as human beings. While we have no opinion about this research either way, we figure it's a good enough reason to believe that people and mushrooms were meant to be together. What better way than this dish? It is wonderful. As an aside, this filling can be used for mushroom ravioli as well, if you have a flair for homemade pasta.

PASTRY
1 8-oz package Cream Cheese
½ pound unsalted Butter
¼ teaspoon salt
2¼ cups Flour

FILLING
3 TBS unsalted Butter
1 large Onion, finely chopped
½ pound fresh Mushrooms (mix of White, Shiitake, Crimini, Portobello), sliced
¼ tsp Thyme
½ tsp Salt or to taste
½ tsp freshly ground Pepper
2 TBS Flour
¼ cup Sour Cream
1 Egg, beaten, mixed with about 1 TBS water

FOR PASTRY: Knead together all ingredients into a dough, then roll into a ball. Wrap in waxed paper and chill 4 hours before using.

FOR FILLING: Melt the butter in a skillet over medium heat and cook the onions until browned. Add the mushrooms and cook about 3 minutes. Add the thyme, salt and pepper, and stir to blend. Sprinkle the flour over the top, then stir in the sour cream, stir again, and cook a moment longer until thickened.

While mushroom mixture is cooking, roll out the dough on a lightly-floured surface to a little less than a 1/8" thickness. Cut into 4" rounds. Place some of the filling into each – too little and the turnovers will seem doughy, too much and they'll pop open. Fold the dough circle over the filling, lightly brush the inside edge with the beaten egg wash, and press the edges together lightly with the tines of a fork. Poke the tines through the top once to let the steam out when they're cooking.

Brush each turnover with a little of the egg wash and place them on the top rack of the oven.

Bake at 325º for 10 minutes or until browned.

Garlic Macaroni and Cheese

PREP: 15 minutes   COOK: 25 minutes   SERVES: 8

How do you make a nearly perfect all-American comfort food even better? Add roasted garlic, that's how. We thought it would make a difference, but we didn't realize how much better it is. The garlic takes the dish to an entirely new level. As Bob's daughter Taylor says, it's "Bomb-diggety". That's a technical culinary term for WOW!

1 TBS Butter
¼ cup Seasoned Breadcrumbs
1 (8 oz) box Macaroni or small shells,
  cooked according to package instructions
1 bulb Roasted Garlic
¼ pound American Cheese
¼ cup Milk
¼ pound Sharp Cheddar Cheese, grated

In a skillet over medium to medium-high heat, melt the butter, then quickly toast the breadcrumbs in it until just lightly browned. Remove from heat. While the noodles are still warm from cooking, stir in the roasted garlic. In an 8" casserole dish, alternately layer the noodles and cheese until both are used up. Pour in the milk.

Place the casserole on the lower rack and bake 20 minutes at 350°. Stir briefly, and top with the toasted breadcrumbs, then move to the top rack and bake for an additional 3-5 minutes or until breadcrumbs are lightly browned.
Serve with roasted tomatoes.

Roasted Garlic

2 bulbs Garlic
  Olive Oil
  Salt

Cut the top ½" off the garlic bulbs, exposing the garlic cloves while leaving the rest of the skin on. Set the bulbs in a pie plate close together and drizzle them with the olive oil.

Roast on the lower rack of the SuperWave for 20 minutes at 425°. Squeeze bulbs to extract roasted garlic from skin.

Coconut Cilantro Couscous

PREP: 5 minutes   COOK: 5 minutes   SERVES: 4

We like this dish because it has a subtle, satisfying fullness of flavor that complements lighter fare such as chicken and fish. On top of that it is quick to prepare.

1 cup Chicken Broth or Chicken Bouillon
1 tsp Butter
¾ cup Couscous
½ cup Coconut, shredded
¼ cup Cilantro, chopped
¼ cup Peanuts for Garnish

Mix all ingredients but the peanuts in an oven-safe 8" or 10" casserole dish and place on low rack of SuperWave Oven.

Cook at 375° for about 5 minutes.

Let stand for 2 minutes, fluff, garnish with peanuts and serve.

Roasted Asparagus

PREP TIME: 5 minutes   COOK TIME: 20 minutes   SERVES: 4

1 Bunch Asparagus, preferably on the thinner side
¼ cup Olive Oil
Salt and Pepper

Place the asparagus in a large bowl or 13 x 9 baking dish. Pour olive oil over and toss to thoroughly coat the asparagus stalks. Sprinkle with salt and pepper to taste.

Place asparagus on rack in oven. Roast at 350° for 20 minutes or until ends are dark but not charred, and stalks are just barely crisp.

Green Rice

PREP: 12 minutes   COOK: 15 minutes   SERVES: 4

We like to change things up a bit. This dish is more a savory rice pudding than anything else, but serves the purpose of mac and cheese on the family dinner plate.   If you want to throw your family a real curve, add some chipotle or Serrano peppers to this before you bake it.

1 ¾ cup cooked Rice
2 Eggs
1 cup Milk
½ cup Olive Oil
1 small Green Pepper, finely chopped
½ small Onion, finely chopped
½ cup minced Parsley
½ cup grated Cheese (Parmesan or Asiago are good choices)

Place the rice in a large bowl. In a second bowl, mix together the eggs, milk, olive oil, green pepper, onion, and parsley. Add to the rice and mix thoroughly.

Pour into a shallow, buttered or greased 8" or 10" casserole dish. Top with the grated cheese. Bake on the lower rack of the SuperWave at 325º for 15 minutes.

Spanakopita Puffs

PREP: 12 minutes   COOK: 7 minutes   SERVES: 4

½ cup Butter
1 Egg, beaten
½ Onion, chopped
2 oz Cream Cheese, room temperature
¼ pound Feta Cheese
20 oz Frozen Spinach, thawed and squeezed dry
1/8 tsp Black Pepper
1/8 tsp fresh Oregano or Basil, minced
1 Pkg Puff Pastry or refrigerated Croissant Dough or pre-formed pastry shells

Thoroughly mix all but dough and ¼ cup of the Butter in a bowl and refrigerate, uncovered, for 1 hour. Remove from fridge and spoon ½ cup filling into the pastry shells. If using refrigerated croissant or crescent dough, separate each section along perforations, using one section for the bottom and one, flipped, for the top. Seal edges of shells with fork.

Brush with remaining butter and bake on the top rack of the SuperWave for 7 minutes at 375º.

Roasted Root Vegetables

PREP: 10 minutes   COOK: 15 minutes   SERVES: 4

Root vegetables are defined as any of those vegetables which grow as roots or tubers. They are great sources of energy and nutrition, as well as being versatile and delicioius. Boldly flavored , this vegetable blend compliments any meal.

4 Carrots, cut into 1-inch pieces
2 Red Onions, cut into 1-inch pieces
2 medium Parsnips, peeled and cut
   into 1-inch pieces
5 cloves Garlic
¼ cup Olive Oil
1 TBS Balsamic Vinegar
1 TBS fresh Rosemary, chopped fine
2 tsp salt

In a large bowl, toss the vegetables with the other ingredients. Spread the vegetables in one layer across the racks of the SuperWave.

Roast for 15 minutes at 450°. Turn vegetables with tongs at about the 8 minute mark, if you'd like them crispy on both sides.

Gingersnap Squash

PREP: 7 minutes   COOK: 13 minutes   SERVES: 2

If the name of this isn't enough to get you to try it, think about this: Can you imagine any kid in the world who wouldn't eat something that had cookies crumbled over it? We didn't think so. We not only love the idea of this, but we fell in love with the flavor. You will too.

1 medium Squash (Butternut, Crookneck or Acorn), peeled and cubed ½"
1 Green Onion, chopped fine
2 TBS Honey
2 TBS Brown Sugar
3 TBS Lemon Juice
¼ tsp Cinnamon
6 Gingersnap Cookies, crushed

Place the cubed squash in a shallow 8" baking dish or casserole.

In a separate bowl, mix honey, brown sugar, lemon juice and onion until smooth. Pour over the squash and top with the gingersnap cookies.

Set the 8" casserole inside a 10" casserole filled halfway with water and set on the bottom rack of the SuperWave. Bake for 13 minutes at 400°.

Baked Goods

Never-Fail Cheese Souffle

PREP: 15 minutes   COOK: 20 minutes   SERVES: 4

Oh boy, is this a great recipe! The art of a perfect soufflé is a dying one in America. But that need not be the case. This recipe Bob developed makes it easy to see why a great soufflé has for decades been the benchmark of culinary achievement. It is light while being intensely flavorful and, as all worthy soufflés do, it satisfies without bulk.

4 TBS Flour
¼ tsp Salt
dash of freshly ground Pepper
½ cup Mayonnaise
4 TBS Milk
1 cup grated Cheese (Cheddar, Swiss, Monterey Jack)
4 Egg Whites
Dash of Cream of Tartar

Grease four 3" ceramic ramekins, especially around the top collar.

In a mixing bowl, gently stir the flour, salt, and pepper into the mayonnaise. Don't over mix. Add the milk slowly, stirring until smooth. Stir in the cheese gently but thoroughly.

Beat the egg whites until stiff. Add in the cream of tartar while beating. Gently fold the mayonnaise mixture and the egg white mixture together until blended (don't overdo it). Pour into the ramekins and set them on the low rack of the oven.

Bake at 325º for 20 minutes or until the soufflés have risen and browned. Serve immediately.

Quick Coffee Cake

PREP: 15 minutes   COOK: 15-20 minutes   MAKES: one coffee cake

There are few pleasures as fine as setting yourself up with a rich cup of coffee, the Sunday New York Times and a warm slice of this coffee cake fresh out of the Superwave Oven. It makes one appreciate the joys of civilized living.

1 beaten Egg
½ cup Sugar
¾ cup Milk
2 TBS Butter, melted
1 cup Flour
½ tsp salt
2 TBS Baking powder

TOPPING:
½ cup brown Sugar
1 tsp Cinnamon
½ cup chopped Nuts
1 tsp Flour
2 TBS melted Butter

In a bowl, combine the egg, sugar, milk, and butter. In a second bowl, sift together the flour, salt, and baking powder.
Add the dry ingredients to the wet and mix wel
Place the batter into a shallow, greased 10" tart
dish or pie pan. For the topping, combine all the
ingredients in a bowl and stir lightly to mix into
small, crumbly consistency, then spread across
the cake. Bake on the lower rack of the

SuperWave at 375° for about 15-20 minutes, or
until a toothpick inserted in the center of the ca
comes out clean.

Applesauce Cake

PREP: 15 minutes   COOK: 10-14 minutes   MAKES: one cake

This is as much a quick bread as it is a cake, but it turns out so moist it's hard to call it anything else. We like it made with chunky applesauce if you can find it. The chunks of apple, bits of raisin and nuts make for a fantastic textural contrast to the spice cake they are baked into. Top it with whipped cream or even cream cheese frosting to gild the lily if you are so inclined.

½ cup Butter
2 cups Sugar
1 large Egg, beaten
1½ cups <u>thick</u> Applesauce
2½ cups Flour
½ tsp Salt
½ tsp each of ground Cinnamon, ground
    Cloves, ground Allspice
1 cup Raisins
½ cup chopped Nuts
2 tsp Baking Soda dissolved in ½ cup
    boiling Water
½ cup of Applesauce for filling (optional)

In a large bowl, cream together the butter and the sugar. Add the beaten egg, beat again. Add the applesauce and mix well.
In another bowl, sift together the flour, salt, and spices. Add this to the wet ingredients and stir slightly to mix. Add the raisins, nuts, and the baking soda water. Blend well.
Pour ½ the mixture into a greased 8" or 10" cake pan. Bake on the lower rack of the SuperWave at 350° for about 12-14 minutes, or until a toothpick inserted in the center comes out clean. Repeat the baking process with the second ½ of the batter. If desired, spread the ½ cup of applesauce on the top of one of the cakes, and place the second cake on top, making a layer cake.

Orange Twists

PREP: 30 minutes (not including rising)   COOK: 12 minutes   MAKES: 16 large twists

This is a shortbread style "cookie" that is marvelous for parties and gatherings. As far as we can remember, Mom only ever made these at the holidays, but they are certainly tasty enough to serve all year 'round.

½ **recipe Sweet Dough**
1/3 **cup Sugar**
1 **TBS grated Orange Rind, minced very fine**
¼ **cup melted Butter**
1-2 **tsp Orange Juice, room temperature**

Knead the dough until smooth and roll out to ¼" thickness. Combine the sugar and orange rind in a bowl and mix well. Melt the butter with the orange juice and brush the dough with it. Sprinkle over with half of the orange sugar. Fold the dough into third. Roll out again to a ¼" thickness, then repeat step two with the rest of the melted butter/orange juice. and the orange sugar. Cut the dough into strips, then twist each strip a full twist. Place the twists on a greased or non-stick baking sheet. Bake at 325° for 12 minutes.

Variations: These yummy twists can be made with a variety of citrus. Try substituting lemon, lime or grapefruit. You can also give them a darker, richer flavor by using brown sugar instead of white sugar. Or try them without citrus at all. Substitute 1-2 tsp of cinnamon for the rind and juice, again using brown sugar instead of white. You might also want to sprinkle with a bit of ground cloves as well, but just a pinch.

Standard Sweet Dough

2 **packages dry Yeast**
¼ **cup lukewarm Water**
1 **cup hot Milk (but not boiled)**
1/3 **cup Butter or Shortening**
½ **cup Sugar**
1 **tsp Salt**
2 **Eggs, beaten**
5 **cups Flour, sifted**

In a small bowl, dissolve the yeast in the water. In a second bowl, add the butter, sugar, and salt to the warmed milk and stir until dissolved. Combine the yeast water and the eggs in a large bowl. Beat in 2 cups of the flour until smooth. Add the remaining flour, one cup at a time, beating it in completely, until you have a soft dough. Place the dough on a floured board and knead until smooth and elastic. Form into a loose ball. Brush the top of the dough ball with a little cooled melted butter. Place in a container and cover, letting it rise until it doubles. Once doubled, the dough is ready to use.

Scones

PREP: 15 minutes   COOK: 5 minutes   MAKES: 12 3" scones

Each February, Paul collects sap from maple trees near his home and boils it down over a roaring fire to produce a few precious quarts of smoky-sweet Pennsylvania maple syrup. Most maple trees give sap that render one gallon of syrup for every forty gallons of sap collected.

Needless to say he is particular about how he uses it. This is one recipe that always gets made, though. One of these and a cup of earl gray tea will sustain a person on even the most inhospitable winter day.

2 cups Flour
¼ tsp Baking Soda
2½ tsp Baking Powder
1 tsp Salt
¼ cup Sugar
2/3 cup Milk
1 Egg, beaten
1/3 cup Butter or Shortening

Sift the dry ingredients together in a mixing bowl. Mix the egg with the milk and slowly mix into a dough. Cut in the shortening.

Turn the dough out onto a lightly-floured surface. Knead the dough by hand for 1-2 minutes. Pat the dough down to about ½" thick and cut into 12 equal rounds or wedges. Place the rounds on the racks of the oven and bake at 400º for about 5 minutes, or until the scones are lightly browned.

Variations: *Try adding ½ cup of currants or raisins to the dough before patting it down and cutting into rounds or wedges. Or instead of currants, add in ½ cup of chopped nuts. Or if you'd like both just do a ¼ cup of each. We also like the idea of topping the scones with a rich jam, like blueberry or strawberry. Or, if you'd really like to go all out, top them with the following Maple Glaze:*

Maple Glaze

½ cup Confectioner's Sugar
2 tsp hot Water
1/8 tsp Maple-flavored Extract

Mix all ingredients together in a bowl and whisk until smooth. Spread or drizzle over the scones.

Tip: *This glaze is particularly good if you add chopped walnuts to the scones.*

Cherry Puffs

PREP: 12 minutes   COOK: 10-15 minutes   MAKES: 4 puffs

As closely related to old-fashioned English tea cakes as anything you are likely to find, these cherry puffs are delicious. Take a few to work to share during your coffee break or invite the ladies over for tea and treats. Your friends and coworkers will be delighted.

2 TBS Butter
½ cup Sugar
1 Egg, well beaten
½ cup Milk
1⅓ cups Flour
¼ tsp Salt
2 tsp Baking Powder
½ tsp Nutmeg
1 cup Cherries, drained
Whipped Cream

In a bowl, cream the butter and sugar. Add the egg and the milk and blend well.

Sift together the flour, salt, baking powder, and nutmeg, then add the dry ingredients to the wet and mix well. Add the cherries and stir gently to combine.

Pour the batter into individual, greased 3" ramekins or similar-sized ceramic molds.

Place on the top rack of the SuperWave and bake at 350° for 10-15 minutes. Serve with whipped cream.

Hot Pepper Corn Bread

PREP: 10 minutes   COOK: 15 minutes   MAKES: one 8" cornbread

1 cup Corn Meal
1 cup Flour
½ cup Sugar
½ tsp Salt
1 cup Sour Cream
½ tsp Baking Soda
2 TBS Butter, melted
2 Eggs, well beaten
2-3 Jalapeno Peppers, chopped

In a large bowl, mix the first six ingredients. Add the sour cream mixture to the dry ingredients and mix well. Do the same with the melted butter. Add the eggs and beat the entire mixture well. Pour into a greased 8" or 10" pan. Place on the lower rack of the SuperWave and bake at 350° for about 15 minutes, or until a toothpick inserted into the center comes out clean.

Sweet Things

Scratch Chocolate Cake
with Peanut Butter Frosting

PREP: 15 minutes   COOK: 8-10 minutes   MAKES: one cake

Long before H.B. Reese dipped peanut butter in chocolate and created his famous cup, people were probably combining these two great flavors. And why not? The two are brilliant together, and never any better than in this recipe.

½ cup boiling Water
¼ cup Butter or Shortening
1 cup Sugar
¼ cup Cocoa
1 ½ cups Flour
½ tsp Salt
½ tsp Baking Powder
½ tsp Baking Soda
1 Egg, beaten
½ cup Sour Cream
½ tsp Vanilla Extract

In a large bowl, mix together the water, butter, sugar, and cocoa. Beat until the sugar is completely dissolved.
Sift together the flour, salt, baking powder, baking soda. Add half the dry ingredients to the wet and mix well. Add the egg, sour cream, and vanilla and mix again. Add the remaining flour and mix well.

Pour into a greased cake pan and bake at 350° for 8-10 minutes or until a toothpick inserted into the center of the cake comes out clean.

Peanut Butter Frosting

1 ½ cup Confectioner's Sugar
3 TBS scalded Cream or Evaporated
   Milk
2-3 TBS smooth Peanut Butter

Mix all ingredients in a bowl until well-blended and smooth. Spread on cake.

Tip: If the frosting is a bit thick and stiff, thin i with a little additional cream, but add the cream in only a tablespoon at a time, so it doesn't thin too quickly or too much.

Caramel Bread Pudding
with Spiced Whiskey Sauce

PREP: 10 minutes   COOK: 20 minutes   SERVES: 8-10

When we worked together in the restaurant, we would sometimes make up a pan of this bread pudding using stale bread and rolls from the day before. You wouldn't think bread pudding was sophisticated restaurant fare, but it always sold out. We think it's because the caramel flavor is s rich and satisfying and the whiskey sauce dresses it up for any cuisine. At any rate, it's excellent.

4 cups stale Bread, diced
3 cups warm Milk
¼ tsp Salt
3 Egg Yolks
½ cup Brown Sugar
2 TBS Maple Syrup
1 tsp Vanilla
½ tsp Nutmeg
¼ tsp Cinnamon
¼ cup Raisins (whole) or
** Walnuts, chopped**

Dissolve salt in milk and soak diced bread in the mixture until absorbed (about 10 minutes). Meanwhile, mix egg yolks, sugar, syrup, vanilla, spices and beat well. Pour the egg mixture over the bread and stir them lightly until well blended. Place in an 8" baking dish set inside a 10" baking dish filled with water on the bottom rack in the SuperWave. Bake at 350° for 15 minutes. When firm, remove from oven and allow to stand for 5 minutes before cutting. Drizzle each slice with Spiced Whisky Sauce and serve.

Spiced Whiskey Sauce

PREP: 3 minutes   MAKES: 1 ½ cups sauce

1 cup Confectioner's Sugar
5 TBS Butter, softened
1/8 TBS Salt
½ tsp Cinnamon, ground
¼ tsp Clove, ground
1 tsp Vanilla
1 TBS Bourbon Whiskey
¼ cup Heavy Cream

Beat Butter until light.
Slowly add confectioner's sugar until completely incorporated.
Add salt, cinnamon, clove, vanilla and whisky and beat well, adding the cream in at the very end until smooth.
Refrigerate for at least 20 minutes before serving.

Southern Sweet Chocolate Pie

PREP: 20 minutes   COOK: 25 minutes   MAKES: 10-12 servings

Our grandparent's housekeeper Alice hailed from Richmond and knew what she was doing with baking. She kept her secrets to herself but she sent us this one recipe. We had to laugh when we found she used ingredient amounts like "a little bit", "a handful", "enough", and "a little less than a coffee cup". It took us a while to figure it out, but here it is. Thanks Alice.

1 4-oz package sweet Cooking Chocolate
¼ cup unsalted Butter
1 2/3 cups Evaporated Milk
½ cup Sugar
3 TBS Cornstarch
1/8 tsp Salt
2 Eggs
1 tsp Vanilla Extract
1 unbaked frozen 10" Pie Shell
1 1/3 cups flaked Coconut
½ cup chopped Pecans
Whipped Cream for garnish

In a nonstick saucepan over low heat, mix the chocolate and butter, stirring constantly until well blended. Remove from heat and gradually blend in the evaporated milk.

In a mixing bowl, mix together the sugar, cornstarch, and salt. Add the eggs and vanilla and beat until blended. Pour in the chocolate mixture and stir until well blended. Pour this mixture into the pie shell. Combine the coconut and the pecans and sprinkle them over the filling.

Place the pie on the bottom rack of the SuperWave and bake at 375º for 25 minutes or until the pie is puffed and browned. Cover the pie loosely with foil for the last 5 minutes if the topping browns too quickly. Cool in the refrigerator for at least 4 hours before serving. Garnish with dollops of whipped cream.

The World's Best Cobbler

PREP: 20 minutes   COOK: 20 minutes   MAKES: one 8" round or square cobbler

When our family moved back east from Colorado, we settled in the recently developed suburbs northeast of Wilmington, Delaware. Our new neighborhood sat on the edge of what was once an enormous peach orchard. Long abandoned, the overgrown trees were still producing good fruit, so when the peaches came in, we picked all we could. Best of all, we could always count on Mom to make this cobbler from what we picked. It's wonderful.

1½ cups Flour
2 tsp Baking Powder
2 TBS Sugar
¼ tsp salt
½ cup unsalted Butter
1 Egg
½ cup Milk
2 to 3 cups fruit (Apples, Blueberries, Peaches, Pears or a mix), peeled, cut into 1/8"-thick wedges
3 TBS Sugar
3 TBS Flour
2 TBS unsalted Butter

Make the dough first, so it can rest while you do the other parts of the recipe. Sift together the flour, baking powder, sugar, and salt. Add the ½ cup of butter and mix to the crumb stage. In a separate bowl, beat the egg with the milk and add it to the flour mixture and mix until a dough forms. Set aside. Prepare the fruit. In a large bowl, mix the fruit with the 3 tablespoons of sugar and the 2 tablespoons of flour. Pour the fruit into an 8" round or 8" square ceramic baking dish, and dot here and there with the 2 tablespoons of butter, broken up.

Cover the fruit in the dish with the dough, place on the lower rack of the oven, and bake at 375° for about 20 minutes. Serve hot.

Variation: We probably don't have to tell you this, but you'll miss one of the great mouth experiences if you don't top a serving of this cobbler with a large scoop of vanilla ice cream.

Chocolate Drops

PREP: 30 minutes (not including refrigerating)   COOK: 10 minutes   MAKES: 2 dozen

Every Wednesday at one o'clock all year 'round, Mom and her friend Olivette would sit down to watch their "story" and have a sweet, which was invariably something chocolate. This was one o their favorites.

1 cup Butter
2 cups Sugar
2 Eggs, beaten
4 squares melted semi-sweet
  Baker's Chocolate
2 cups Flour
2 tsp Baking Powder
  granulated Sugar

In a medium bowl, cream together the butter and sugar. Add the beaten eggs and mix well.
Slowly add the melted chocolate (but don't let it be too hot when you add it), and blend everything together well.
In second bowl, sift together the flour and the baking powder, then add it to the butter mixture and mix well.

Store the batter in the refrigerator for at least 12 hours before baking.

When ready to bake, form the batter into balls the size of marbles, and roll each one in the granulated sugar before placing in a nonstick 8" round cake pan.

Place the pan on the top rack of the SuperWave and bake at 350° for about 10 minutes. Let cool.

Butterscotch Cookies

PREP: 20 minutes (not counting chilling)   COOK: 10 minutes   MAKES: 2 dozen

2 cups Brown Sugar
½ cup Butter
2 Eggs
3 ½ cups Flour
1 tsp Cream of Tartar
1 tsp Baking Soda
  Butterscotch Morsels

In a large bowl, cream the butter and sugar together. Add the eggs and mix again.
Sift together the flour, cream of tartar, and baking soda Add this mixture to the butter/sugar mixture and blend well into a creamy batter.
Form the dough into 2 rolls, wrap in wax paper and chi for about an hour. lice into ½" thick cookie rounds and place in an 8" round nonstick cake pan. Place the pan on the bottom rack of the SuperWave and bake at 375° for about 10 minutes or until just browned. During the last minute, drop a butterscotch morsel in the center of each cookie.

Meringue Cookies

PREP: 15 minutes   COOK: 5-7 minutes   MAKES: 20 2" cookies

1 Egg White, stiffly beaten
1 cup Brown Sugar
1 TBS Flour

In a bowl, gradually add the brown sugar to the beaten egg white. Fold in the flour. Drop by the teaspoonful onto a wax or parchment paper-lined cookie sheet or cake pan.

Bake on the top rack of the SuperWave at 250° for about 5-7 minutes. Let them cool before removing them from the pan, as they are very delicate and until they cool are likely to crush easily. You might want to have two of the cake pans to work with and alternate them as you're working through the batch of dough.

Variations: You can play around with this recipe in dozens of different ways....Add a cup of nuts to the mixture before baking....Add a teaspoon of cinnamon to the mixture....Add a teaspoon of vanilla or almond extract to the mixture...Or a teaspoon of peppermint extract for the December holidays. It really is up to you, and the possibilities are endless.

"Light As A Feather" Gingerbread

PREP: 15 minutes   COOK: 10-12 minutes   MAKES: one 8" gingerbread

Gingerbread was developed by medieval monks as a treatment for indigestion. It was considered good for one's constitution and people were encouraged to eat it regularly. Sure....let's go with that. Now, this recipe might not be medicine, but it is light on the palate and oh, so tasty.

1 cup boiling Water
½ cup Butter or Shortening
½ cup dark Brown Sugar
½ cup dark Molasses
1 Egg, beaten
1 ½ cups sifted Flour
½ tsp Salt
½ tsp Baking Powder
½ tsp Baking Soda
¾ tsp ground Ginger Powder
¾ tsp ground Cinnamon

Pour the boiling water over the butter or shortening and stir with a fork until the butter is dissolved. Add the brown sugar, molasses, and egg, and mix well.
Sift together the flour, salt, baking powder, baking soda, ginger, and cinnamon. Add this mixture to the wet ingredients and beat until smooth.

Pour into a greased 8" square pan. Bake at 350° for 10-12 minutes. Allow to cool before serving.

Variation: This gingerbread is great when topped with the Never Fail Frosting.

Never Fail Frosting

1 cup granulated Sugar
¼ tsp Salt
½ tsp Cream of Tartar
2 Egg White, unbeaten
3 TBS Water (or orange or apple juice, if you want to really spice it up)
1 tsp Vanilla Extract

Place all ingredients together in the top of a double boiler. When water in double boiler comes to a boil, place the top pan over the bottom and turn off the heat. Beat the ingredients until it achieves a spreadable consistency.

Apple Crisp

PREP: 10 minutes   COOK: 10-15 minutes   MAKES: one 10" crisp

We have a rule of thumb about desserts. Go with the apple. We have long discovered when in restaurants that no matter how beautiful the rest of the desserts are, it's going to be the apple thing that tastes the best. We know...there is a chocolate lobby out there screaming to the contrary right now, but when you taste this recipe you'll understand why we prefer to, "Have the apple."

5-6 cups peeled and thinly-sliced Apples
1 cup Flour
¾ cup Sugar
1 tsp Baking Powder
¾ tsp Salt
1 unbeaten Egg
1/3 cup melted Butter
Whipped Cream or Custard Sauce

Place the sliced apples in the bottom of a greased 10" tart baking dish.
In a bowl, place the flour, sugar, baking powder, salt, and the egg. Mix with a fork until crumbly. Sprinkle this mixture over the apples.
Pour the butter over all. Place on the bottom rack of the SuperWave and bake at 350º for 10-15 minutes, until crisp on top. Top each serving with whipped cream or custard sauce.

Variations: This can be made with pears as well.

Custard Sauce

PREP: 15 minutes   COOK: 15 minutes   MAKES: about 4 cups

4 cups Milk
1 cup Sugar
3 Eggs, beaten
1-2 tsp Vanilla Extract

In a heavy saucepan over low heat, cook and stir milk and sugar until sugar is dissolved. Remove from the heat. Stir in a small amount of hot milk mixture into eggs; return all to the pan, stirring constantly. Cook and stir until mixture reaches 160º or is thick enough to coat a metal spoon.
Remove from the heat; stir in vanilla. Cool to room temperature, stirring several times. Transfer to a bowl; press a piece of waxed paper or plastic wrap on top of custard. Refrigerate. Serve over gingerbread or pound cake.

Chocolate Whoopie Pies

PREP: 10 minutes   COOK: 10 minutes   MAKES: 18 small pies

Everyone loves whoopies. How can you not? They have big size and a big flavor to match, so everyone is happy. Watch your kids' eyes light up when you bring a tray of these to the table after dinner. Wonderful.

2 cups Flour
1 cup Sugar
½ tsp salt
2 Egg Yolks
1 tsp Baking Soda
5 TBS Cocoa
1 tsp Baking Powder
½ cup soft Butter
1 cup Milk
½ tsp Vanilla

In a bowl, sift the dry ingredients together. Then add the rest the rest of the ingredients and mix well. Using a tablespoon, drop a tablespoon each of the mixture onto greased round cookie sheets or small, round, metal cake pans.

Bake on the lower rack of the SuperWave for 7 minutes at 350° or until set, not crisp. Put the pies together sandwich style, using two pies with filling in the middle. Makes 18 sandwiches treats.

Whoopie Filling

12 oz. Philadelphia Cream Cheese
1 stick Butter (8 tablespoons)
1 TBS Vanilla Extract
6 cups Confectioner's Sugar
** (slightly more if needed)**

In metal bowl, whip together butter and cream cheese, preferably with an electric mixer. Add the vanilla and mix again until smooth. Mix in the confectioner's sugar slowly, whipping until smooth and airy and all is incorporated.

Pumpkin Whoopies

These are basically hand held pumpkin rolls, and boy, are they good. We make them every fall and enjoy every bite. You will too.

In a metal bowl, beat the eggs yolks, brown sugar, and oil together until smooth. Add the pumpkin and all the dry ingredients. Mix again until well-blended. Drop by the tablespoon onto greased round cookie sheets or small, round, metal cake pans.

Bake on the lower rack of the SuperWave at 375° for 7 minutes or until the whoopee rounds are golden brown. Sandwich with the filling and serve.

2 Egg Yolks
2 cups Brown Sugar
1 cup Vegetable Oil
1 tsp ground Cloves
1 tsp ground Cinnamon
1 tsp ground Ginger
1 tsp Salt
1 tsp Baking Soda
1 tsp Baking Powder
1 tsp Vanilla Extract
2 cups Pumpkin, cooked and pureed, or canned
3 cups Flour

Index

Resources for
an Uncertain Future

Resources for an Uncertain Future

**Papers presented at a Forum
marking the 25th anniversary
of Resources for the Future,
October 13, 1977, Washington, D.C.**

Charles J. Hitch, editor
Lewis M. Branscomb
Harrison Brown
Robert W. Fri
Paul W. MacAvoy
William H. McNeill
Edward S. Mason
Charles L. Schultze

Published for Resources for the Future
by The Johns Hopkins University Press
Baltimore and London

Copyright © 1978 by The Johns Hopkins University Press
All rights reserved. Manufactured in the United States of America.

Library of Congress Catalog Card Number 77-18378
ISBN 0-8018-2105-3
ISBN 0-8018-2098-7 paper.

Contents

Foreword

The papers published in this brief volume were prepared for presentation October 13, 1977, at a forum marking the 25th anniversary of the founding of Resources for the Future (RFF) as a non-profit research and educational organization. Since 1952 there has been a growing public awareness of resource and environmental problems and an enormous increase in the importance of these problems on the agenda of public policy. RFF has contributed substantially both to the public understanding of these issues and to the clarification of policy issues through the publication of some two hundred studies, as well as by speeches, seminars, and testimony by staff members. The purpose of the forum was to appraise, from a number of perspectives, the resource and environmental outlook for the United States during the next twenty-five years in the light of events of the recent past. What are offered here are informed opinions on selected issues rather than the kind of research that is customarily associated with RFF publications. We hope that the questions raised here will help stimulate discussion as we search for better ways to cope with an uncertain future.

Foreword

The views expressed here, as in all RFF publications, are those of the authors and are not to be interpreted as those of RFF staff members, officers, or directors.

Charles J. Hitch
President, Resources for the Future

Washington, D.C.

Resources for
an Uncertain Future

Resources in the Past and for the Future

Edward S. Mason

Dean Emeritus, Harvard University, and Honorary Member of the
Board of Directors of Resources for the Future

My introduction to natural resource problems
came during World War II, when I was employed
as an economist in the Office of Strategic Services. For an economist in a wartime intelligence
agency, one of the chief tasks was estimating the
industrial and military production of the Central
Powers, principally Germany. It became a continued and increasing source of astonishment to
see how Germany, with relatively small supplies
of metals and minerals, could achieve such large
outputs of trucks, planes, munitions, and other
war matériel—outputs that expanded steadily
from 1939 to 1944, despite growing losses from
aerial bombardment. The answer to this was fully
revealed only after the war, largely as a result of
the investigations of the U.S. Strategic Bombing
Survey. It then became known that, although the
consumption of copper in the United States during the war years was ten times that in Germany;
of tin, twenty times; of manganese, ten times; of
nickel, forty to fifty times; and of other scarce
metals in proportion, Germany ended the war

with larger stocks of most of these metals than she had in 1939.

How was this accomplished? It was done mainly by the substitution of relatively plentiful metals for relatively scarce ones; the redesigning of equipment in order to eliminate or to curtail scarce metal requirements; the extensive collection of scrap; and the paring down of civilian requirements.[1] Of particular interest were the technological possibilities of substitution that were involved in the redesigning of equipment. At the beginning of 1942 railway locomotives contained, on the average, 2.3 metric tons of copper, but by the middle of 1943 this had been reduced to 237 kilograms, or about one-tenth of the original amount. Early in the war the building of a submarine required 56 tons of copper; later this was reduced to 26 tons. The use of alloy steel was virtually eliminated from railway car construction, and iron radiators were substituted for copper radiators in all motor vehicles. In the use of ferro alloys, relatively plentiful vanadium and silicon were substituted for the less plentiful alloys. Vanadium was substituted for molybdenum in gun tubes under 21 centimeters in length. Nickel was replaced by vanadium in gun tubes under 10.5 centimeters in length. In addition, new processes were devised for working lower-grade ore supplies, such as chrome sources in the Balkans. And, of course, the very large quantities of scrap that exist in all highly industrial societies were assiduously collected and utilized.

It cannot be said that the German manage-ment of raw materials shortages was accom-plished without cost. Obviously, labor inputs per unit of output were increased, and in some cases, no doubt, a certain loss in the quality of finished products was unavoidable. But it must be em-phasized that, despite the scarcity of essential materials, the German war effort was not limited by a shortage of raw materials and that this very considerable transformation and substitution was accomplished in a relatively short period. During a war emergency, of course, cost con-siderations are of relatively small importance. In Germany, technology was set free to do what could be done without worrying too much about price incentives and disincentives. Nevertheless, one could not help but be impressed that scarcity is a relative term, to be interpreted only with all the possibilities of substitution in mind.

After the war I wrote a number of articles on materials and national security,[2] and I suppose that these led to my next venture in the natural resources area, my membership on the Presi-dent's Materials Policy Committee, the so-called Paley Commision, which published its final re-port, Resources for Freedom, in 1952. In those days you remember that everyone was for free-dom—,"Full Employment in a Free Society";

economic growth in a free society; and in a Harvard football program, the leading article was entitled "Football in a Free Society."

The Paley Report

The Paley Commission was appointed during one of those recurring periods in American history when a potential shortage of industrial materials seemed imminent. Consumption of materials during wartime had been stupendous, and whether or not the United States could look forward to rapid economic growth unimpeded by material shortages and what, if anything, we needed to do for security reasons, seemed to be questions worth investigating. Interest in these questions was currently heightened by the very large increase in materials prices occasioned by the Korean War. President Truman's letter of January 22, 1951, admonished the commission, "We cannot allow shortages of materials to jeopardize our national security nor to become a bottleneck to our economic expansion. The task of the Committee, therefore, will be to make an objective enquiry into all major aspects of the problem of assuring an adequate supply of production materials for our long-range needs and to make recommendations which will assist me in formulating a comprehensive policy on such materials."[3]

The commission did indeed make a large number of recommendations but, in the main, these were ignored as the postwar fear of materials shortages gave way to a comfortable complacency. The principal impact of the commission's report lay in its findings and methods of analysis, and the report is, perhaps, as interesting for what it ignored as for what it emphasized. Its primary tool of analysis, in dealing with prospective adequacy of supplies, lay in the concept of real costs. What would constrain economic growth was not, in the commission's view, the physical limits of discoverable supplies but the real costs of making those supplies available; that is, the real costs, measured either in the labor or capital inputs per unit of output or in the prospective price of materials in relation to changes in the general price level. If real costs were the constraint, an examination of the material limits to growth required more than a forecast of rates of consumption and a knowledge of existing and potential reserves. It required a study of the possibilities of substitution within a flexible price system and an estimation of the possibilities of technological innovation. A substantial part of the commission's report, therefore, was devoted to technology and to the possible effects of technological change on the redesigning of products and processes, the recycling of materials, the excavating of leaner ore bodies, and other applications bearing on what might happen to the real costs of materials.

The commission undertook a careful study of what had, in fact, happened to the real costs of mineral and agricultural raw materials during the period 1900–50 and came to the conclusion—surprising to most people—that for all groups, except forest products, the trend of real material costs was downward; and for many groups, strongly downward. So far from being a constraint on economic growth the declining costs of material inputs had been a growth accelerator. This effect was further enhanced, as the commission discovered, by the fact that the value of all material inputs constituted a persistently declining share of the GNP. As Barnett and Morse later calculated, the percentage of value added to the GNP, accounted for by the consumption of extractive production, mineral, and agriculture, declined from 45 percent in 1870 to 14 percent in 1957. As they point out, this decline over nearly a century marked, more or less, the transition from a preindustrialized society, oriented to raw materials production and consumption, to a highly industrialized society, oriented toward the fabrication of materials.[5]

It might have been thought that, since the commission found raw materials production and consumption constituted a declining share of total output and since the real cost per unit of materials output had been persistently falling, they would have concluded that all was well. Indeed, there was a tendency to come to this conclusion, but it was severely undermined by considerations of future uncertainties and the desire, at all costs, to be responsible statesmen. So the commission concluded, "Real costs of materials production have for some years been declining, and this decline has helped our living standards to rise. In this Commission's view, today's threat in the materials problem is that this downward trend in real costs may be stopped or reversed tomorrow—if indeed this has not already occurred."

In fact, as later studies have shown, this decline in the real costs of materials production and extraction per unit has continued, with minor exceptions, up to the present. Barnett and Morse carry the calculations to 1957, and Nordhaus computes the relationship of the prices of ten important minerals to the price of labor from 1900 to 1970. Their computations indicate "that there has been a continuous decline in resource prices for the entire century." And Nordhaus adds, "Unless all materials suddenly hit a kink in the cost curve at the same time, it seems unreasonable to foresee a drastic runup of the costs of minerals relative to wages in the near future." [6] Given continued progress in technology, a flexible price system, and adequate supplies of energy, the general conclusion must be that a shortage of industrial materials is not likely to be, at least in the foreseeable future, one of our serious resource problems. I shall return to the question of energy shortly.

The report of the Paley Commission also emphasized the increasing dependence of the United States on foreign sources of raw materials. Based on its estimates of production and consumption of materials other than food and gold, it found that in 1900 the United States had a 15 percent surplus available for export, as against a deficit of 9 percent and a prospective deficit of 20 percent in 1975. Later investigations of U.S. foreign trade in raw materials indicate an interesting situation.[7] For a very small number of materials, including platinum, mica, chromium, and strontium, the United States is completely dependent on foreign sources of supply. This was true in 1950, and it is also true today. With respect to other raw materials, the United States—with the exception of oil, gas, iron ore, and zinc—is not any more dependent in 1975 than it was in 1950. Imports of iron and zinc could be replaced by domestic production and substitution without a large increase in costs. It is a different matter for oil and gas. The fact is that the American raw materials trade is now heavily influenced by oil imports and food exports. This will have a considerable bearing on the future energy position of the United States and on the future food situation in the rest of the world.

The Environmental Considerations

As I suggested earlier, the report of the Paley Commission is interesting not only because of its findings, but because of what it ignored. It says nothing about the desirability of protecting the environment in the course of meeting American materials requirements. One could defend the commission by saying that it was not asked to consider this question. However, a more perspicacious group of enquirers—particularly a group that emphasized the importance of real costs—might have asked themselves the question, How much will an adequate protection of the environment add to the cost of meeting materials requirements? In fact, it was not asked, and, in 1950 few, if any, were asking this question. Enquiry into the costs of environmental protection burgeoned only in the last fifteen to twenty years, and RFF has been a leader in this enquiry.

One would have to go back to the conservation movement which flourished between 1890 and 1910 in order to discover the initial impetus in this country for environmental protection. This was a political movement with objectives as disparate as saving the forests, destroying the monopolies, and maintaining Anglo-Saxon supremacy. Its economic analysis was practically nonexistent, though it did emphasize the importance of sustained yield in renewable resources. The best it could do in defining the meaning of conservation was to say that it meant a "wise use of resources." Since almost any program could be accommodated under this rubric, we can sympathize with President Taft's dictum, "A great many people are in favor of conservation no matter what it means."[8] Despite the fuzziness of the concept, however, many in the conservation movement had a feeling for environmental values of a very modern character. The American frontier was disappearing, urban congestion was increasing rapidly, the farm population had begun to decline, forests were being raped, and rivers and lakes had become polluted. No general solution to these problems existed, other than to "prevent waste," but there is no doubt that a high value was assigned to environmental protection.

The question is, How much will it cost us to maintain an adequate protection of the environment? Or, to put the query in the form in which it currently engages attention, How much of our growth rate will need to be sacrificed in order to maintain the air and water standards, the urban noise levels, and the availability of natural resources amenities that we are willing to live with? There have been some attempts to estimate, in terms of their percentages of the GNP, the costs of maintaining, particularly, certain air and water standards, but at best they are educated guesses. There are difficulties in specifying the procedures to be used in pollution abatement and estimating the costs thereof; there are difficulties in defining the objectives sought to be attained; and there are difficulties in relating the cost and benefits of pollution abatement to a meaningful measure of national income or the GNP. According to the venturesome United Nations study, *The Study of the World Economy*, directed by Leontief and others, countries with per capita incomes above $2,000 would need to spend from 1.4 to 1.9 percent of their GNP for pollution abatement to attain air, water, and waste disposal standards specified by U.S. agencies.[9] For these purposes, the United States spent 1.6 percent of its GNP in 1974, but how effective this was in attaining government-specified standards is not fully known. According to the Survey of Current Business, "In 1974 non-farm business firms spent $5.6 billion for new plant and equipment to abate air and water pollution and dispose of solid waste. . . ." This amounted to 5 percent of total new plant and equipment spending.[10] Allen V. Kneese estimates that by spending 5 percent of their GNP from now to the end of the century, "Developed countries should be able to reduce the amount of residuals discharge to their environment to a small fraction of what it is now." [11] How this small fraction would relate to U.S. standards is not indicated. Five percent would appear to be on the high side of existing estimates of expenditures needed to maintain government-specified standards. These estimates appear to converge on a figure of, perhaps, 2.5 percent during a catch-up period of a few years, followed by a reduction to, perhaps, 2 percent a year. How such expenditures would affect the GNP, as it is conventionally calculated, is unclear, but such a rate of expenditures on pollution abatement would obviously mean a considerable shift in patterns of consumption. We would consume less of some goods and services than we are accustomed to consume but would enjoy access to a purer environment. Welfare might well be improved whatever happened to GNP as conventionally calculated. The estimates we have cited presumably do not cover the costs of providing other urban and natural environmental amenities. All that we can be sure of is that there is a real conflict between the objectives of economic growth, as conventionally conceived, and protection of the environment.

It is, in fact, rather early to make overall estimates of the cost of environmental protection. The problem needs to be broken down into its constituent parts, in order to devise better measures of social costs and social benefits; and a greater effort must be made to learn how to establish a political consensus on the objectives to be reached before we attempt to strike a balance between growth and protection of the environment. There seems little doubt that this is the natural resource problem of today and the immediate future. We encounter it on every side, in the siting of electrical plants, the laying of pipelines in Alaska, the disposal of nuclear wastes, the problem of automobile emissions, the pollution of lakes and rivers, urban noise levels—one could go on indefinitely. Resources for the Future has worked effectively on many of these problems, and I would suppose this will constitute its central activity for a long time to come.

The Myth of Scarcity

Despite the dicta of the Club of Rome, we are not facing scarcities of industrial materials. So far as I can see, we do not even confront a danger of rising costs of these materials for the next century at least, and probably longer. On the world scene, the principal scarcity problem is finding enough food to feed a continuously expanding population, and, indeed, if there are no limits to population growth, it may be an insoluble problem. I see no serious scarcity problems for the United States as a whole, assuming that we can adopt a sensible energy policy.

Edward S. Mason

A striking feature of the energy situation in the United States is that while we are confronted with impending shortages of such highly convenient energy sources as oil and gas, there are not practical limits to alternative supplies—coal, nuclear power, and, with improved technology, other sources—which can be made available over time and perhaps at no considerable increase in real costs. At present rates of consumption and using known technologies, it is probably true that the United States and the world, despite additional discoveries, will run out of oil and gas early in the twenty-first century. If consumption continues to increase at the 1970's rate of 6 percent per annum, exhaustion of available supplies that can be made available with existing technology, and at something like the present price, would come sooner. Exhaustion, however, will not take place at a precise date, with ample supplies before that date and zero supplies afterwards. Instead it is likely to be a protracted process, with rising prices shutting off certain areas of consumption. It should not be beyond the wit of man to prolong the availability of gas and oil by confining their use by strict economies to areas in which there are no convenient substitutes. Unimpeded market forces would, in the course of time, accomplish this purpose, but the process could be facilitated by governmental action, including differential taxation of the uses that need to be discouraged.

This is to view the situation from the demand side and over the relatively short run. In the long run it is possible that improved technology can make available at something like current real prices the very large quantities of natural liquid and gaseous hydrocarbons that are known to be below the surface of the earth. It is possible. But, until more is known of these potentialities, a sensible energy policy must primarily emphasize economizing on supplies that are amenable to conventional methods of extraction.

When oil prices were quadrupled in 1973 because of OPEC, the world, including the United States, took a large, and probably irreversible step away from low-cost energy toward a condition in which energy prices will be persistently higher. In the United States the full effects of that step, however, are not as yet worked out. Government controls still maintain a distinction between old and new oil, and natural gas is still being sold in producing states at prices substantially higher than gas being sold for interstate shipment. This situation cannot last for long. President Carter's energy proposals, if accepted, will eliminate some of these anomalies and, even without government action, market forces within a few years could bring the prices of energy from different sources into some kind of equilibrium. This equilibrated system of prices will provide energy in the United States and elsewhere at a substantially higher cost than pre-1973 costs.

But, given time to bring energy sources other than oil and gas into effective production, it may well be at costs that need not be subject to further substantial increases. Assuming that we can bridge the time gap involved in developing these sources, without falling prey to an attempt by OPEC to maximize its short-run monopoly profits, the price of oil is likely over time to move at levels close to the costs of alternative sources of energy. The money price of oil will presumably continue to increase along with inflation in the prices of other goods.

But the real cost of energy to the United States will depend on the cost of expanding coal production, the cost of increasing nuclear energy with existing technology, and the costs of developing energy from other sources with improved technology. There will, of course, be manifold adaptations in use, as well as in production processes, but, so far as I can see, there need not be very large increases in the average real cost of different energy resources for the United States. What happens to energy costs, of course, will be an important determinant of the real costs of other materials, since the extraction of metals from leaner ore bodies and the recycling of materials substantially increases demand for energy.

The fact that the United States as a whole does not, in my view, confront serious scarcity problems should not be taken to mean that particular regions do not confront such shortages. Clearly, the principal one is the shortage of water in the Southwest and the High Plains. It should be obvious by now that the limits for irrigated agriculture in the West and Southwest have been reached, if not passed, and that if the growing cities of the area are to have enough water, it will have to be at the expense of local agriculture. A proper pricing of water could do much to accomplish this objective, while a sensible recycling of water can substantially increase its availability. Local shortages have always affected the location of industry and population. Heavy water-using industries cannot be sited in areas without streams, and citrus fruits cannot be grown in the Rocky Mountains; but this does not mean that the nation's resources cannot provide adequate food, clothing, and housing for its population into the indefinite future. The fact that not everybody can live in the Sun Belt can hardly be said to constitute a natural resource limitation to national growth.

The Real Issues of Externalities

In the natural resource area the shift away from problems of scarcity toward the interrelation between growth and the protection of the environment has led to new developments in economic and political analysis. In economics, the concepts of public goods and externalities have been brought out of the cupboard and subjected to renewed scrutiny. In politics, the problem of achieving at least a practical course of action, if not consensus, in an area beset with conflicting interests and discordant values, has taken on new dimensions.

The concept of public goods is at least as old as the science of economics. In Adam Smith's time the emphasis was on the economies of scale, which dictated that the provision of certain goods and services lay beyond the capacity of private enterprise and must therefore be undertaken by the state. The services of defense had to be provided on a national scale; making roadways, sewage facilities, and parks available to all on a community basis was much cheaper than to provide these facilities to each household privately. The surrounding atmosphere did not come into the discussion as a public good, and nobody talked about the ecosphere, the biosphere, or any other kind of sphere.

Although economies of scale still have relevance for certain types of public goods, primary attention has shifted to the problem of congestion. No one can be excluded from the use of public good because it is impossible to charge a price for the use of the goods or because it is socially undesirable to do so. Although Samuelson defines pure public goods as goods for which additional consumption by one individual does not diminish the amount available to others,[12] not many public goods are "pure." In fact, national defense may be one of the few examples. A more typical example of a public good is a public highway on which, at least during rush hours, additional use by one or more individuals definitely seems to diminish the space available to others. Or, to take another example, the use of a stream by a pulp mill will certainly diminish the downstream access to pure water. Most of the problems of environmental protection arise from the impossibility of excluding other users of the parks, public beaches, and other so-called public amenities.

As Rothenberg observes, "Depending on the nature of the public good, a differing but rather wide range of users may be accommodated with no perceivable deterioration of quality. Each good has a capacity or threshold." [13] Beyond that, quality deteriorates with increasing congestion. Pollution is a particular form of congestion in which the users are divided into those who pollute and those who are the victims of pollution. The current analysis of public goods centers on these various consequences of congestion.

The other ancient concept that has been resurrected and put to new uses by the emergence of environmental problems is that of "externalities." An external effect occurs when the costs or benefits of an activity are not limited to the individual or firm responsible for it but are shared by outsiders. The early discussion of externalities concentrated, for some reason or another, on bucolic examples. The bees of farmer A collect honey from the flowers of farmer B, with subsequent loss to farmer B; lumbering operations on a hillside lead to excessive runoffs and floods, damaging properties in the valley; cinders from locomotives set fire to adjacent wheat fields; or straying cattle trample crops on other people's land. These stories of the birds and bees, formerly thought useful in conveying the facts of life to our children, seem to have seized the imagination of nineteenth-century writers on externalities. When Milton Friedman lumps the whole problem of externalities under the innocuous phrase "neighborhood effects," he seems to be thinking in much the same way.[14]

When one looks, however, at the extensive pollution of air and water resources, interference in the radio spectrum, and the struggles in the West for access to public lands and public waters, it is difficult to sweep the problems of externalities that are involved under the rug of "neighborhood effects." We are accustomed in our youth, or at least I was, in our reading and at the movies, to learn about the struggles between sheepmen and cattlemen for access to public grazing lands. This conflict was an early example of congestion, or is it pollution? These struggles pale, however, before the cutthroat competition for scarce water in the West. Public goods and externalities are at the heart of the problem. Again, RFF has been at the forefront in exploring the modern applications of these concepts.

Environmental concerns have also greatly extended the dimensions of political analysis. If the primary concern of politics is who gets what, when, where, and how, one welcomes an opportunity to analyze the process of sharing environmental resources and amenities among competing interest groups, or states, or communities concerned with employment or economic growth. There is little doubt that adequate protection of the environment will markedly increase the role of government in society and test the ability of representative government to achieve a workable concensus of conflicting claims of growth and environmental protection and to devise efficient procedures to implement this concensus. This does not mean that all the advantages of the impersonal market need be thrown away. Indeed, one of the advantageous ways of dealing with certain types of environmental protection is through pollution charges, leaving the polluter a certain measure of freedom in the choice of ways and means. But, even here, it will have to be the government that assesses the requirements and fixes the charges, while the most serious issues involved in choices between growth and environmental protection will have to be decided, not in the market, but in the political arena.

What is now happening in the world suggests that natural resource problems, including possible conflicts between growth and protection of the environment, raise issues not limited to the United States or any other single country. Smoke emitted from high stacks in Britain comes down as acid rain in Norway; in their pursuit of whales, Japan and the Soviet Union may rid the world of these interesting mammals. Tuna fishermen are decimating our stock of dolphins. The potential mineral resources of the seabed are a current source of fierce international debate. The uneven spread of arable land and mineral resources across the surface of the earth creates opportunities for international trade and investment that need to be sensibly exploited if the benefits of growth are to be widely shared. Resources for the Future has begun to explore a number of these areas and is likely to find, in the course of these explorations, plenty of problems to engage its attention in the next quarter-century.

Footnotes

[1] This conclusion and the following figures are taken from E. S. Mason, "American Security and Access to Raw Materials," *World Politics* (January 1949), p. 148.

[2] In addition to the above-mentioned article, see E. S. Mason, "Raw Materials, Rearmament and Economic Development," *Quarterly Journal of Economics* (August 1952); and "An American View of Raw Materials," *Journal of Industrial Economics* (November 1952).

[3] President's Materials Policy Committee, *Resources for Freedom*, vol. 1 (Washington, GPO, 1952), p. 12.

[4] A principal finding of the Paley Commission report (President's Materials Policy Committee, vol. I, p. 4), was that "the value of the material stream rose by only half as much as the national output; (1900–1950) services were beginning to become a larger proportion of the goods and services that made up this output, and more value was being added to materials by successively higher fabrication as time went on."

[5] H. J. Barnett and C. Morse, *Scarcity and Growth; the Economics of Natural Resource Availability* (Baltimore, Johns Hopkins University Press for Resources for the Future, 1962), p. 233. Workers in extractive industries (including agriculture) as a percentage of all U.S. workers declined from 52 percent in 1870 to 11 percent in 1957. Barnett later reexamined this proposition, bringing the calculations of materials cost up to 1970 (*Scarcity and Growth Revisited*—Mimeograph, 1972). He found that, in general, the record of declining costs continues.

[6] W. D. Nordhaus, "Resources as Constraints on Growth," *American Economic Review* (May 1974), p. 24.

[7] Compare with H. Landsberg, "Energy and Materials; How They Differ in the International Context," *Engineering and Mining Journal*, vol. 177, no. 10 (October 1976), pp. 63–71. RFF Reprint 135, 1976.

[8] *Outlook* (May 14, 1910), p. 57.

[9] United Nations, *The Future of the World Economy* (Preliminary report, 1976), pp. 29–30.

[10] *Survey of Current Business* (July 1975), p. 15.

[11] A. V. Kneese, *Economics and Environment* (Baltimore, Penguin Books, 1977), p. 252.

[12] P. A. Samuelson, "The Pure Theory of Public Expenditures," *Review of Economics and Statistics* (November 1954).

[13]J. Rothenberg, "The Economics of Congestion and Pollution: An Integrated View," *American Economic Review*, vol. 9, no. 2, p. 14.

[14]M. Friedman, "The Role of Government: Neighborhood Effects," reprinted in R. and N. Dorfman, *Economics of the Government* (New York, Norton, 1972), p. 202.

Resources and Environment in the Next Quarter-Century

Harrison Brown

Director, Resource Systems Institute, East—West Center, and Member of the Board of Directors of Resources for the Future

Before speculating about what the next twenty-five years might have in store for us, it is of some importance to examine the major concerns about resources which were relevant twenty-five years ago and compare them with those of today.

Yesterday

Resources for the Future was born in an atmosphere of technological optimism. In spite of the Korean War, which had recently been concluded, there was also a great deal of optimism concerning America's position in the world and the state of the American economy. Thanks in part to the Marshall Plan the economies of Europe and Japan were recovering rapidly. The cold war was in full swing, and defense industries were booming. There seemed little doubt that the Soviet Union would be contained militarily regardless of her nuclear capacity. The level of affluence in the United States was unprecedented and growing rapidly. Never before had a large population of human beings been so well off.

Attitudes concerning nonrenewable resources can be judged by the thinking at the time concerning energy, the "ultimate resource." I remember attending a conference at Northwestern University in early 1951 on the subject of world population and future resources. Great concern was expressed at the conference about population growth, but little alarm was expressed about future supplies of energy, despite the fact that the United States had crossed the line only three or four years earlier to become a net importer of liquid fuels.

Robert E. Wilson, then chairman of the board of the Standard Oil Company of Indiana, spoke eloquently on this subject.[1] His main conclusion was that "America can continue to have plentiful supplies of liquid fuels at reasonable cost for many generations to come if she will do just three things, namely, preserve freedom of enterprise, freedom of research, and adequate incentives." He recognized that U.S. fuel requirements could not be met indefinitely from domestic crude oil resources and suggested, with considerable confidence, that we could probably turn first "to imported petroleum; second, to natural gas; third, to oil shale; fourth, to coal; fifth, to tar sands; sixth, to agricultural products; and seventh, to air, water, and sunlight." He placed great stress upon the future importance of imports and emphasized that, fortunately, "the great bulk of all Western

Hemisphere reserves and about half of the probable Near East reserves are in American control." He expanded the view that the trend toward imports is "a healthy development, but the healthiest thing about it is that natural economic conditions determine it, and not someone else's ideas of what should be done." Wilson was not specific as to what he meant by "natural economic conditions," nor did he suggest that such conditions might be related to the fact that Middle Eastern oil was selling for $1.50 a barrel at a time when the incremental cost of the oil at dockside was about $0.10 a barrel. He did say, however, that "the richness of some of the Middle East resources is not widely appreciated."

The report of the Paley Commission appeared in 1952, and it, too, was generally optimistic about the future of oil and of energy. The report stressed that it would be prudent for us to import relatively low-cost oil, thus saving our own. There was no implication that there would be a supply problem in the near future, stressing that "there is as yet no evidence of failure to discover resources adequate to support growing production."[2]

There were, of course, some individuals who were less optimistic; for example, M. King Hubbert, who had published his classic paper, "Energy from Fossil Fuels," in 1949.[3] Application of the principles which he enunciated suggested that crude oil production in the conterminous

United States might well peak about 1970. But even this possibility gave little cause for alarm. Quite apart from the availability for import of huge quantities of inexpensive crude oil in South America and the Middle East, we knew that the United States was endowed with vast quantities of coal and oil shale, which our technological prowess would enable us to convert to liquid fuels. Furthermore, we were confident that electricity generated from nuclear energy was very close to being economically practicable. There appeared to be little need to worry.

At the Mid-Century Conference on Resources, which was sponsored by Resources for the Future in 1953, experts divided sharply into two groups. The larger group was composed of the technological optimists—who their protagonists dubbed "cornucopians." The smaller group was composed of those who held strong conservationist views and who sincerely believed that our rapidly expanding consumption of nonrenewable resources was leading industrial societies, and the world, toward disaster. Now, twenty-five years later, we realize that in many ways both groups were right—and that they were, in a sense, arguing about the wrong problems.

The conservationists of twenty-five years ago were the forerunners—indeed, one might say the founders—of today's school of thought concerning the limits to growth. In 1953 Samuel Ordway,

Jr., in his *Resources and the American Dream*,[4] summarized the views of this group as follows:

Levels of human living are constantly rising with mounting use of natural resources.

Despite technological progress we are spending each year more resource capital than is created.

If this cycle continues long enough, basic resources will come into such short supply that rising costs will make their use in additional production unprofitable, industrial expansion will cease, and we shall have reached the limit of growth.

It is interesting to note that in this great cornucopian–conservationist debate there was no mention of the possible global environmental consequences of human actions, with the single exception of the effects of improper land use.

Today

A quarter of a century has now passed, and in that period we have seen the U.S. resource position change in dramatic ways that had not been foreseen. As had been anticipated by some persons, proved reserves of crude oil in the conterminous United States peaked about 1960, and production peaked about 1970. Although the Paley Commission forecasts for total U.S. petroleum demand in 1975 were remarkably accurate, the estimate of total U.S. production turned out to be high by one-third, and the estimate of imports was low by a factor of between two and three. All signs now point to a continued rapid growth in U.S. dependence upon imports of crude oil.

At the same time, there has been a widening cleavage between the rich and the poor countries brought about, in part, by rapid growth of affluence in the rich ones and rapid population growth in the poor. Most reserves of exportable crude oil are found in developing countries. These countries also possess large reserves of nonfuel minerals which the industrial nations need.

With the proliferation of politically independent national states which take their so-called sovereignty extremely seriously, and with the emergence of OPEC as an effective cartel, the "American control," which was referred to rather confidently by Robert E. Wilson, has in large measure disappeared. Further, there has emerged within the developing countries a deep-seated and increasingly militant antagonism toward the rich ones.

In 1973–74 the industrial democracies reeled from a shockwave: first, the fourfold increase in the price of crude oil imposed by the Organization of Petroleum Exporting Countries (OPEC); and then, the Arab oil embargo. In a brief, three-month period we saw wave after wave sweep through our economies. Even more important, we saw control of access to crude oil used for the first time as a major weapon of war. Almost instantaneously,

Japan did an about-face in her foreign policy with respect to Israel. Western Europe was severely shaken. Great Britain was particularly hard hit, because the embargo began when considerable disruption had occurred as the result of strikes by electrical workers and coal miners.

During and shortly after the crisis of 1973–74, there was much talk about the United States achieving greater energy independence. Now, only four years later, after hearing much talk and seeing almost no action, we appear to be even further from that goal than we were then. We now import well over half of the petroleum we need in the form of crude oil and refined petroleum products. As a result of this, we are running balance-of-payments deficits of unprecedented size. These are increasing despite our efforts to export increasing quantities of agricultural and industrial products and despite the fact that we have greatly expanded exports of expensive sophisticated weaponry—particularly to major oil exporters—with potentially disastrous consequences for world peace.

Major oil exporters have been saving or investing substantial shares of their oil earnings in the United States. Much of the money which has been deposited in U.S. banks has been loaned to Third World countries, enabling them to pay their oil import bills. Nevertheless, there is now considerable danger of defaults on a large scale.

The other industrial democracies currently find themselves in an even more difficult position than does the United States, for they must import even greater amounts of their crude oil. In order to pay for their increased imports, they, too, must export more. As in the United States, these export drives have led to expanded weapons sales, as well as to sales of dangerous nuclear technologies and a major resurgence of protectionism.

At the same time, the tensions between the industrial democracies and the poor nations are increasing in substantial measure because of the rich countries' control of production, investment, and trade. The developing countries seek agreements involving their trade position with respect to about a dozen major commodities, excluding oil, which account for about 80 percent of their export earnings. They demand a higher proportion of the consumer price, and they would like to establish a mechanism for eliminating disastrous price fluctuations. Beyond commodities, they would like to see major relaxation of present restrictions against importation of their manufactured products. They, too, must export in order to pay for their petroleum imports.

In this struggle between the rich and poor nations, OPEC is, for understandable reasons, championing the cause of the poor and is in a position to use two major weapons—oil and money—to achieve this and related goals.

As the struggle goes on, the Soviet Union can afford to wait it out for she is basically self-sufficient with respect to resources. This is an overwhelming geopolitical fact—the ultimate significance of which few of us fully appreciate. To be sure, the Soviet Union has some technical and organizational problems in tapping her considerable oil and gas reservoirs and developing adequate distribution systems from remote areas. But it seems likely that she will solve these problems, while making full use of her unequaled coal reserves. At the same time, she is exporting substantial quantities of petroleum and gas to her energy-poor satellites in Eastern Europe. This, of course, provides her with an element of political control which transcends armies in its power.

Why is it, that in spite of our vast resources of coal and oil shale, our nuclear technology, and our potential for utilizing solar energy, we have not been able to halt the increasing need for petroleum imports? In substantial measure this stems from the incredible inexpensiveness of crude oil and natural gas, as they are priced today. Nothing else can really compete. All alternative energy options require tremendous capital investments, and even when the economics are favorable, a great deal of time is required to reduce new approaches to practicality. Added to this, virtually all possibilities for large-scale power generation have environmental problems associated with them, most of which are probably solvable but costly in both money and time. Further, a mystique has arisen concerning nuclear power which makes it increasingly difficult to build new plants or to operate old ones.

The fact is that we have become "hooked" on crude oil and natural gas and the cost of kicking the habit is substantial.

Tomorrow

The problems that will confront us during the next twenty-five years are clearly formidable. The greatest likelihood is that we will continue on our present course and that the needs of the industrial democracies for imported crude oil will continue to increase. The evidence suggests that world production of crude oil is likely to peak around the year 2000, and a major question will be whether we will be able to cope with this situation, which is not so very far in the future.

But quite apart from our ability to cope with the problem of the beginning of the end of crude oil, we will be called upon to handle a multiplicity of other energy-related problems long before that time. Crude oil is now a recognized weapon of war, no matter whether it will be directed by the Arab states against Japan or the United States for their policies with respect to Israel, or by the United Nations against South Africa for its social policies.

It is of great importance that we recognize fully the vulnerability of the United States, Western Europe, and Japan to major disruptions in the flow of crude oil. We can be destroyed more effectively, and certainly much more neatly in this way, than were we at the receiving end of a massive H-bomb attack. Indeed, the dedicated use of the oil weapon could kill us as a functioning nation. The possibility of its use could lead us to take actions which might be equally disastrous. In my opinion, the United States is in a far more dangerous position today than at any time since the Civil War. Japan and Western Europe are in even more dangerous positions.

Thus, I believe it is essential that the industrial democracies diversify their sources of energy as quickly as possible. This will not be easy because no matter what route is taken, the costs of energy will go up. In particular, capital costs will become very large.

Unfortunately, this is a problem which simply cannot be solved through the free movement of market forces, which would lead simply to continued rapid increases of imports, further increasing our vulnerability. The situation is one in which government must intervene, providing needed incentives and disincentives, as well as guarantees.

How much should we be willing to pay for energy? Are the present economics of energy really functioning for long-term human benefit when such economics make it so attractive for us to consume the greater part of the existing petroleum and natural gas in the world before we learn how to use coal and oil shale effectively?

Clearly, the fairness of a price should be related in some way to the cost of doing business in the absence of the resource. If there were no crude oil available, hydrocarbon fuels would be obtained by conversion of oil shale or coal to synthetic fuels. If the price of crude oil were raised to a level greater than the cost of converting oil shale or coal, and if the price were predictably maintained, there would be little question that conversion plants would be built in profusion.

Of course, when the price of crude oil was raised so rapidly in 1973–74, the consumer nations could not have taken any meaningful action for the simple reason that options other than that of accepting the increased prices (or perhaps engaging in military action) were simply not viable. A great deal of time is required to develop the necessary technology, to accumulate the needed substantial capital, and to build the plants.

If energy sources other than crude oil and natural gas are to be developed and put into operation on a meaningful scale for the generation of power and the production of liquid fuels, the price structure of our various energy resources must be reexamined and drastically altered. Here,

I use the term *price* to include all costs to the consumer including taxes, less government subsidies.

Ideally, the revised price structure and associated guarantees would make oil shale and coal competitive with crude oil and natural gas (both domestic and imported) for the production of liquid fuels and petrochemicals. Nuclear power from fission would be made competitive with coal for the generation of electricity. Solar energy would be made competitive with fossil fuels for space heating and cooling. In this way, all of our major, near-term energy possibilities would be developed and utilized on a substantial scale.

Of course, under such circumstances our energy costs would be greater than they are today, but probably not more than double the current price of imported crude oil. And here we must keep in mind that, even if we do nothing, the price will at least double again anyway as the result of outside forces. How much better it would be for the increases to be under our own control, and on a schedule developed by us!

It is essential that the importing industrial nations—Japan, the nations of Western Europe, and the United States—arrive at a common agreement on energy pricing and on taking artificially higher energy costs into account in the pricing of their manufactured and agricultural products, particularly those for export. To take an extreme case, were Japan to continue with OPEC oil as its primary source of energy, and were Germany to shift primarily to coal and nuclear energy, Japan would, for the time being, have a marked economic advantage. Obviously, some compensatory understanding would be necessary to keep the system from falling apart.

No matter how we handle our energy problems during the next twenty-five years, we must face the fact that the environmental element of the energy equation will become increasingly important. It is difficult to see how reasonable levels of energy self-sufficiency can be achieved in the near term unless nuclear energy is used on a substantial scale, and the environmental problems that would be associated with this are well known. Unfortunately, the mystique which has arisen in most industrial nations concerning the dangers associated with nuclear power has taken on the appearance of a religious war, in which logic and experience have been lost sight of and actions are governed largely by emotions. Reasonableness will not be brought back into the nuclear power picture unless rules are adopted for nuclear power plant siting and generating procedures. It must be made obvious to everyone that accidents which can endanger human life will be rare; large-scale human catastrophe will be virtually impossible; radioactive wastes can be stored safely; and diversion of explosive-grade nuclear materials will be so difficult that it will not be a matter of serious concern. I believe that these goals are technologically and administratively feasible.

Finally, during the next twenty-five years we must come to grips seriously with the problem of the increasing carbon dioxide content of the atmosphere. I suspect that sooner or later it will become necessary for nations to limit their rates of combustion of fossil fuels. This would mean converting to a combination of nuclear and solar power. From a technological point of view, this would certainly be feasible. But in a multinational world, in which each nation guards its sovereignty, how would the rationing of fossil fuel combustion be accomplished?

Indeed, if I were asked to identify the greatest single barrier to the solutions of global resource, environmental, and development problems in the world today, I would necessarily point to the tight grip in which the concept of national sovereignty holds the world's peoples. I suspect that at least another century must pass before this force is no longer dominant. Under the circumstances, we in the United States must come to grips with our resources problems on the assumption that, for some time in the future, we will continue to be a part of an anarchic world.

I have confined my discussion to energy because, given adequate supplies of energy, we need never suffer from lack of nonfuel minerals. I have confined my discussion of energy to those aspects of energy which will be of greatest importance during the next twenty-five years.

We must face the fact that we are living in a period marked by the convergence of several critical trends. In addition to energy, these include growing affluence and population, diminishing resources, expanding weaponry, and the increasing tensions between the rich and poor nations. The time scale for this convergence is about another twenty-five years. If by that time we have not truly come to grips with these problems in a significant way, we will find ourselves in the middle of a crunch to end all crunches.

The way in which we navigate the next twenty-five years will be crucial for the survival of our civilization. The obstacles in our path are numerous and will be difficult to overcome. I am convinced, however, that those obstacles can be overcome and that we can create a new and higher level of civilization. We certainly have it in our power to do so. The real question is, Do we have the political will?

Footnotes

[1]P. K. Hatt, ed. *World Population and Future Resources* (New York, American Book Company, 1952) pp. 212–228.

[2]Report of the President's Materials Policy Commission. *The Outlook for Energy Resources,* vol. III (Washington, G.P.O., 1952) p. 5.

[3]M. K. Hubbert, "Energy from Fossil Fuels," *Science* vol. 109 (1949) pp. 103–109.

[4]S. H. Ordway, Jr. *Resources and the American Dream* (New York, Ronald Press, 1953).

Energy Imperatives and the Environment

Robert W. Fri

Former Deputy Administrator of the Environmental Protection Agency and the Energy Research and Development Administration

Energy and environment is a common enough juxtaposition. In fact, it is rather old hat. But why should I speak of energy *imperatives*? What is imperative about energy? And why not *environmental* imperatives?

To get a handle on this title, let me first examine the nature of the energy problem and its impact on the environment, and then turn to the central issue that the energy—environment trade-off seems to raise. It is, I believe, an institutional issue rather than a technical one.

The Energy Imperative

The energy problem is hard to understand without looking ahead at least twenty or thirty years. Regrettably, few thorough studies of the problem with this time horizon have been published. As a result, I am going to rely on an unpublished study, the Market-Oriented Program Planning Study (MOPPS), undertaken by an extinct Energy Research and Development Administration (ERDA).

It has been, as some of you know, a controversial work. However, I believe it is a thorough, detailed, and balanced analysis and will prove to be a significant contribution to our understanding of our energy situation.

The central point that MOPPS makes is that we do not have a long-term energy shortage, but that we do have an awesome transitional problem —especially in liquid fuels.

Between now and the year 2000, adequate liquid fuel supplies—especially for transportation fuels and petrochemical feedstocks—persist as the central energy problem. Under the National Energy Plan (NEP) ground rules, as originally proposed by President Carter, MOPPS projects that oil imports would amount to 14.2 quads in 1985 and 10.5 quads by 2000. These levels, representing 40 percent of our oil consumption in 1985 and 33 percent in the year 2000, indicate a continuing high dependence on imported petroleum.

But even this relatively high import level may be too optimistic, because the forces driving up the demand for liquid fuels by the year 2000 are hard to resist and may push the demand higher than even MOPPS projects. Transportation is one such force. The demand for gasoline and diesel fuel is likely to rise sharply after 2000, if not before, because, by then, increases in miles driven simply overwhelm all our efforts at conservation. MOPPS projects a 30 percent increase in demand for these fuels between the years 2000 and 2010. Of course, this sharp rise could occur earlier.

Another such driving force is the demand for petrochemical feedstocks. Feedstocks necessarily rise with industrial growth, going from 7.8 quads in 1985 to 11.5 quads in 2000. Within this 50 percent overall growth, liquid demand triples. In principle, natural gas could substitute for liquid fuels as a feedstock. But, owing to gas shortages today, industry is turning increasingly to liquid fuels. As a result, the substitution will be deferred, and liquid fuel demand will stay high.

A final force behind the liquid fuel demand is old housing in the Northeast, where both fuel switching and meaningful conservation measures are exceedingly difficult to achieve.

These forces suggest, if anything, a continuing higher demand for liquid fuels. But even if we cope successfully with such forces, other events could exacerbate our problem. If, for example, electricity demand does not slow markedly from historical rates, industry fails to convert to coal, or our conservation efforts falter, we must turn at least in part to liquid fuels to take up the slack.

Thus, the odds are quite high that the liquids problem will be worse than what the aggregate figures show. It would not be unreasonable to expect added liquid fuel import deficits of 1.5 quads in 1985 and 10 quads in 2000. In case of such deficits, imports would rise to 42 percent of our total oil demand in 1985 and to 49 percent in 2000. These figures, incidentally, are consistent with those projected by the excellent report of the Workshop on Alternative Energy Strategies (WAES).

What about our other energy supplies? Coal certainly presents a more tractable problem than liquid fuels, simply because we have lots of it. The problem here centers around the ability of the market to absorb more coal, even though there are serious questions about our ability to mine it in the first place. Between 1978 and 2000, the utilities' consumption of coal may rise from 8.8 to 20 quads—a large but attainable increase. Industrial use, on the other hand, must quadruple— from 3.7 to 15.8 quads. This is a formidable, and perhaps unattainable, target.

Nuclear power shows similarly large growth rates—assuming the uranium is there. Nuclear power now generates 1.9 quads of energy, and by 2000 should produce nearly 20 quads if the pressures on coal mining are to be kept in bounds. To reach this target, however, nuclear power would have to capture 60 percent of the new power plant market, and that is far higher than its current penetration.

Gas is, interestingly enough, less of a problem. Although we have curtailments today, our natural gas resources are very large, if we are willing to pay the price to top them. Indeed, at a price we can obtain immense sources of gas from coal, the geopressurized zone, or other exotic sources. The problem we face here is one of timing. MOPPS estimates that, in 1985, our gas supply could run anywhere from 3 quads short to 6 quads long. By 2000, the deficit could be 6 quads, and the surplus could be 12 quads. The actual figure depends on how fast we move to free up our gas resources. Thus, with natural gas, the problem is less one of adequate resources than of near-term producibility.

Exotic energy sources—solar, geothermal, and the like—will produce significant energy by the end of the century. MOPPS estimates 0.5 quads in 1985 and 3.8 quads in 2000. Yet, even in 2000, this amount accounts only for 3 percent of total demand. The prospect is encouraging, but falls short of being our energy salvation.

Finally, there is conservation. The total demand for energy in MOPPS is 94 quads in 1985 and 118 quads in 2000. These levels are quite low, lower than those of the NEP, in fact, and they represent savings of 15 or 20 percent over business as usual. However, the failure of this aggressive conservation program has serious consequences. Failure in the industrial sector puts enormous strains on coal use, and in the transportation sector, on liquid fuels. Neither problem is affordable.

Earlier, I said that we do not have an energy shortage. Having just enumerated several energy problems that certainly sound like shortages, let me explain what I mean. I think that the energy imperative can be boiled down to these propositions:

- First, we are running out of oil, and that is a serious problem. But we have vast resources of shale, and of coal for liquefaction. It is imperative to use them.
- Second, we have large coal resources and large potential markets for them. It is imperative to make those markets real. The same can be said of nuclear resources.
- Third, natural gas is not a dying industry, but one in transition to a plentiful, but much higher-cost product. It is imperative that both the resource and economic transition be made as quickly and as painlessly as possible.
- Fourth, conservation is imperative, period.

The Environmental Response

So much for the energy imperative, what now of the environment? Fortunately, there is a recent environmental analysis of the NEP done by ERDA that allows us to be fairly precise about the environmental response to the energy imperative. And there is good news and bad news.

There is good news of a sort, anyhow; the situation is not so bad as you might think. For example, the report projects that all air pollutants will increase somewhat between 1985 and 2000 but suggests that three of five criteria pollutants will remain well below 1975 levels. Similarly, four of five major water pollutants will drop significantly from 1975 to 2000, with suspended solids dropping by 88 percent.

And energy becomes less of a factor in the overall pollution control problem. Generally, pollution control costs will drop from 2.1 to 1.1 percent of the GNP by 2000. And the energy component will drop even more sharply, from 43 percent to 31 percent of the total.

In short, the environmental impact of the NEP is not so bad. And I could end my comments at this point if it were not for two things:

- The NEP does not solve the energy problem, and, if it did, its environmental impacts would be large.
- It is the NEP's reliance on coal that is the source of all the bad news in ERDA's environmental report.

Let me take up the coal question first. Coal is the dominant source of the pollutants that do not decrease. The ERDA report estimates that, even with best available control technology (BACT), emissions of sulfur oxides in the year 2000 will exceed the 1975 levels by 20 percent, and coal combustion is the source of 80 percent of these emissions. Nitrogen oxide emissions will rise 70 percent above 1975 levels, with coal contributing 40 percent of these emissions. In water, total dissolved solids will increase by about 7 percent; in 1975 coal contributed 26 percent of this pollutant but will produce 42 percent in 2000.

However, pollution is only one type of environmental insult. Energy use of land will rise to over 10 million acres by the year 2000, 94 percent of which will be due to coal production. Depending on the region of the country, this represents from 0.5 percent to 3.6 percent of the total land area. Solid wastes, mostly from coal, will rise from the current rate of 100 million tons to over 700 million tons by 2000. And water use for energy will increase from 2 million to 11 million acre-feet per year. Energy use of water rises from 2 percent to 10 percent of our total consumption, and after the year 2000, it will only get worse.

Thus, the use of coal, as envisioned by the NEP, has serious environmental impacts. But worse, the NEP is a limited plan. By looking only as far as 1985, it does not solve the energy problem—nor, for that matter, does it expose its true magnitude. And when we look to the end of the century, it is easy to see that the energy solution requires us to rely on two environmentally intrusive resources—shale and even greater amounts of coal.

I have already mentioned the effects of relying on coal, but shale is a new story. Each quad of shale produces 37,000 tons of sulfur oxide, 140 millions tons of solid waste, and the process uses 37,000 acre-feet of water. We need 10 to 15 quads of liquid fuels to close our import gap. As a percentage of national figures, the airborne emissions and water use connected with shale oil production is small, but that of solid wastes is enormous. Unfortunately, all this impact is not national—it occurs in two counties in Colorado and a couple in Utah.

Indeed, the energy insult on the environment is highly regional. The big loser, as we all know, is the Rocky Mountain region. Under the NEP, this region receives a disproportionate share of strip-mining, mine drainage, suspended-solids runoff, solid waste production, water consumption, energy-dedicated land use, and sulfur oxide production. Thus, we cannot conclude that the NEP or MOPPS, or any other energy projection is environmentally benign.

The Tradeoff

I am afraid that I have taken you on a rather breathless tour of some new statistics. But from it all, a couple of central conclusions emerge. First, it seems clear to me that we risk exhausting our environmental resource long before we will exhaust our energy resource, unless we begin to act differently. We cannot really allow the pollutants most dangerous to our health—sulfur, nitrogen oxides, and dissolved chemicals—to persist above today's levels. Already, our air and water resources have been effectively exhausted by these pollutants. Nor can we risk the land and water use of an ever-expanding energy industry.

Second, we can conclude, I think, that energy is an imperative—or at least more of an imperative than is our environment. The forces responsible for the energy imperative are some of our most cherished national goals. It is not greed that causes our liquid fuels problem, but respectable economic growth, the inexorable growth of even energy-conservative transportation, and the age of our residences. Coal is needed for even modest industrial growth and electricity production. We must promote conservation, but not so fiercely as to slow economic growth markedly. We must not fall into the trap of saying, "Pull in the gangplank, I'm already aboard."

And so there is a conflict, a profound one. And the real issue is, How do we equip ourselves to manage this conflict for the balance of this century? What policies, and, more important, what processes and institutions must we build to carry us into the twenty-first century if we are not to exhaust our environment as we exploit our nearly inexhaustible energy resources?

I do not pretend to have the answer. But I am persuaded that the policies, processes, and institutions of today are strikingly ill-suited to provide the answer. Let me give you a few examples.

First, our energy policy simply lacks the breadth of view to resolve the energy problem compatibly with the protection of the environment. The NEP, even before it ran into congressional headwinds, looked only as far as 1985. Any plans so short-sighted cannot come to grips with the central issues of either energy or the environment. A good example of this is found in the ERDA environmental report as it deals with air pollution. Calculating air pollution loads for the NEP, and for BACT without the NEP, the loads are essentially the same. In other words, the NEP does not make any environmental difference. An energy plan that does not improve the environment is not much of a plan.

Had we an energy policy that truly addressed the environmental problem, we would have more than the energy-economic policy we have. We might have seen an aggressive program to introduce clean, coal-burning technologies—such as fuel cells, solvent-refined coal, fluidized bed combustion, and the like. We might have seen more emphasis on shale oil production *in situ*, which produces desperately needed oil in a more environmentally acceptable way than does above-ground retorting. We might even have seen a turn to coal gasification, both to firm up the long-term gas supply and to give us a way of using coal more cleanly than by direct combustion.

Of course, if we had done these things, we would have paid a price—both in development costs and in the incentives necessary to promote the commercial use of environmentally acceptable technology. But internalizing environmental costs is always expensive, and, in my judgment, always right.

This leads me to the subject of environmental policy. Here, I think, we have a fundamental problem with our approach to pollution control which must be corrected if we are ever to solve energy and environmental problems simultaneously.

The problem is inherent in the approach of setting emissions effluent standards and then enforcing against them. This approach was fine when I was at the Environmental Protection Agency (EPA), because it works well for gross pollution. Six years ago, that is what we had, and it was easy to find and prosecute the polluter who was grossly out of compliance. The violation of standards—any standard—was clear, and any court could see it.

But things have changed. Most industrial polluters, at least, are on the road to compliance, if not there already. And as we get closer to compliance, the standards and enforcement approach works less well. Standards must be more precise since violations are harder to detect, and courts are harder to persuade. As a result, the system has begun to break down, in two ways.

- First, it has become impossibly complex. Standards become more elaborate, and data requirements to prove violations become immense. Equity becomes a problem, leading to such complexities as the nonattainment policy. Frustration with this complexity leads to ideas such as BACT—designed to cut through the maze of regulations by imposing a technological requirement that may not be needed.

- Second, and perhaps more important, the system distorts resource allocation. Standards are imposed externally to the market system, thereby giving up the best resource allocator of all. Worse, disconnecting pollution control from the market system also disconnects it from the energy system. In the long run, I suggest that this broken link will substantially inhibit both energy and environmental solutions.

The alternative is obvious, if not easy to apply. In order to control pollution we need a system of emission or effluent fees. Only such a system truly internalizes environmental costs. Only such a system is likely to optimize resource allocation. It completes the environment–energy–economic linkage. And most important, it is at least as simple as the increasingly unworkable system we now have.

Environmental protection is more than pollution control, of course. It also encompasses the way in which we use our land and water. And here we also have a problem. We plan for land and water use poorly. The fact that we have poor planning systems for land and water use is hardly news. What is news, however, is that we are doing such planning in the absence of good systems and are likely to make some bad mistakes.

A good example is the policy of nondegradation. It is, in plain and simple language, a land use-planning policy. But it is land use planning based on a single objective—the preservation of air quality. It is a noble goal, but hardly the sole one for land use. The longer we pursue it, the more errors we will make.

As long as we do not understand the need to deal comprehensively with our land and water, our environment, and our energy needs, we are destined to continue acting as though every environmental issue were independent of its brothers. We struggle with each problem as though it were the first, and make each policy choice as though it were the last. Then another crisis grabs our attention and we begin again.

Why should it be this way? Why should our energy policies be shortsighted, our pollution control systems be increasingly ineffective, and our land and water use planning be hopelessly inadequate, if not outright counterproductive?

I think that the answer lies in part within the nature of our institutions. For, in the EPA, and now in the Department of Energy (DOE), we have not only created new institutions, but radically different ones. They are problem-solving institutions, created to right a major national ill to the exclusion of all others. And if they stray from their issue too far, their congressional and public constituencies quickly right the course.

Because of their narrow focus and constituency pressure, such agencies behave in odd ways. They discriminate, for one thing. The EPA goes after big polluters and the DOE after big oil companies. They have their hit lists, because they have to show results and stand up to the bad guys.

Such institutions are less than likely to take the long view, for their dedication to their issue is tested daily. Such institutions are not prone to find ways of working through economic incentives; it is too invisible a role. Such institutions probably will not engage in tradeoffs, because someone's ox will get gored. It is instructive to recall the outrage that greeted the notion of a Department of Energy and Environment. But maybe it is what we should have had.

Well, so much for energy imperatives and the environment. There are energy imperatives—resources we must use in order to avoid an energy shortage. Their exploitation may exhaust our environmental resources before our energy sources run dry. And we lack the energy policy, the environmental processes, and the institutions that may be needed to bring energy and environment back into balance.

Perhaps I am too pessimistic. But after nearly six years of close proximity to energy and environmental issues, I cannot be sanguine. Yet, there could be no subject about which an understanding of our resources for the future is more important. Let me commend this institution for attacking the problem twenty-five years ago and wish you success in tackling what promise to be even tougher problems for the future.

Coping with an Uncertain Future—Three Assessments

Historical Perspective
William H. McNeill

Professor of History, University of Chicago

Human history is nothing more nor less than a record of change. It follows that coping with change—the title assigned to the deliberations of this panel—is but another name for the human condition. Problems of food and fuel supply, which loom large in our consciousness today, are not without historical parallels, sometimes remarkably close, as in the case of the seventeenth-century Mediterranean food and fuel crisis that set in with the widespread exhaustion of forests adjacent to that sea. The main difference, it seems to me, is that we in the fourth quarter of the twentieth century are far better informed and can see the disaster coming in a way that earlier generations, similarly threatened, seem not have done. This enhances anxiety in some quarters and induces indifference in others, but it is surely arguable that foresight and anticipation may assist in preparing alternatives and make more likely a successful response to critical shortages. At any rate, the *raison d'être* of this organization, Resources for the Future, consists of that hope.

William H. McNeill

The Consolation of History

If we employ a long enough time scale, humanity's career upon earth looks like the progress of a band of brachiating apes through the forest, leaping from branch to branch, that is, from one ecological niche to another. From time to time, an overloaded branch cracks; bodies sometimes fall to their death; but always, at least so far, new branches have somehow come within reach, and the band swings on.

Our remotest, fully human ancestors began the adventure by climbing to the top of the food chain as the most formidable of hunters. Humankind then proceeded to exterminate many of the large-bodied game animals upon which the hunters were accustomed to prey. This Paleolithic crisis provoked experiments in food production in many different parts of the earth, beginning about 8000 B.C. or so; and in about a dozen localities, sufficiently productive crops and domesticated species of animals were developed to allow the emergence of new and far more populous forms of human society. This change has often been called the Neolithic revolution.

A bit later, the first civilization, based on irrigation agriculture, arose in the floodplain of the Tigris—Euphrates. About a thousand years thereafter, salting of the fields resulting from evaporation brought on a new kind of crisis that required abandonment of the original city sites and relocation of civilized social structures upriver—first, at Babylon, then still further north in Assyria. More significant than this relocation was the gradual emancipation of civilized life from the flood-plains and its domestication on rain-watered land. This occurred about the year 2000 B.C. and made civilization of the Near Eastern variety potentially endemic throughout the relatively broad regions of the earth where soils and climate allowed the production of a food surplus by peasant farmers, using their own muscles and those of a few domesticated animals for the tasks of cultivation.

A couple of thousand years later a new kind of ecological disaster hit wide regions of the by-then-civilized world of Eurasia. I refer to the exposure of large populations to new and formidable epidemic diseases. The resulting die-off in both China and the Roman Empire, where surviving records allow reasonably precise estimates, were severe and, together with barbarian invasions and civil disorders, led to widespread decay of civilized forms of social organization. The resulting Dark Age lasted for several centuries in Western Europe; but in time recovery did come, probably quite as rapidly as recovery from the Paleolithic food disaster. Global history, accordingly, witnessed first a rise of the East, as China attained leadership in almost every aspect of civilized life, and then a rise of the West, when

Europe followed suit and swiftly expanded its range of action over all the world.

Yet Europe's rise was by no means one long uninterrupted record of material progress. Local disasters, sometimes involving setbacks lasting for centuries, abound. The decay of German cities during and after the Thirty Years' War is a familiar example; the collapse of Dutch prosperity under the burden of the French wars is another. The decay of Italian cities after the first decades of the seventeenth century is a less familiar instance, since it was not tied in directly with warfare; but details have recently been worked out by a brilliant cluster of French historians. Of course these disasters were local. In each case, in an adjacent part of Europe, conditions were such that a continued growth of technology, or organizational skill, and of knowledge could and did occur. From sufficient remove, therefore, the whole process looks like a single upthrust, recurrently raising human power and wealth to higher and higher levels.

The consolation of history, then, for those harried men who seek to cope intelligently with the looming food and fuel crisis of the twentieth and twenty-first centuries is short and simple: we are not unique; you are not alone. Human beings have often confronted analogous situations and, so far at least, have always found new ecological niches that, in fact, allowed more people to share the surface of planet Earth than had before been possible.

This is not a trifling consolation, it seems to me, and I strongly recommend Fernand Braudel's famous work *The Mediterranean in the Age of Philip II* as bedside reading for anyone worried about the oil problem we face today—for it was he, more than anyone else, who illuminated the dilemmas facing Mediterranean people and states immediately before and after 1600 when supplies of wood began to run low.

Ambivalence of Our Position

All the same, I would like to also emphasize ways in which our situation differs from what earlier generations faced. As I said already, the first difference is that we know so much. As far as I am aware, earlier ecological–economic disasters were not foreseen; or if foreseen by humble technicians of some sort, their views did not reach, or were not taken seriously, by political and cultural leaders, and accordingly left no trace in available records. Untoward developments were, characteristically, attributed to supernatural action. The Will of God explained everything that happened and may sometimes have discouraged mere human effort to head off disaster. Given the realities of life in a time when vagaries of weather ruled the harvest, and when raids and ravaging by who knew what unfamiliar band of ruffians was an ever-present possibility, any explanation of things that did not emphasize the unexpected and uncontrollable aspect of experience would have been utterly at odds with life as actually lived. It is not surprising, therefore, that divine retribution for past transgression was the only explanation human beings found plausible when some new disaster overtook them. Since the seventeenth century, however, a few European visionaries, calling themselves natural philosophers, propounded the notion of a world machine whose movements were, or ought to be, predictable. Such "scientific" views challenged older, providential interpretations of reality, and govern most of thought today, despite the fact that human experience has yet to be reduced to predictable proportions.

Nevertheless, we are always probing the limits of understanding, and disseminate data relentlessly. We extrapolate and exaggerate and cry "Wolf, wolf!" And when that does not get attention, try something still more shrill in the hope of galvanizing the public into action. Whether this noisy concern for the future will sharpen reactions and improve chances of an effective response when real shortages arise remains to be seen. But we will be conscious of the process as our predecessors seldom or never were; of that we can be sure. I suppose the chances of a successful response are increased rather than diminished by this fact, despite the distractions that competing voices create.

A second difference between our situation and that of any preceding generation facing an impending ecological crunch is likewise ambiguous in its augury for future success. I refer to the fact that the wealthier countries of the world today have pretty well destroyed the old, peasant agricultural class upon which earlier civilizations rested. This meant an enormous increase in efficiency and a rise in living standards. It also means that if the web of exchange that nourishes our cities and sustains our farming should ever come to a halt for as much as six months, the resulting disaster would be enormous. Aforetime, when about four-fifths of the population raised its own food and produced locally almost everything it consumed, cities and civilization could rise and fall and affect the lives of the rural majority only marginally. Consequently, the social basis for rebuilding an urban civilization lay ready at hand, no matter what kind of disaster city folk might experience.

Today it is still true that more than half of humankind exists at a peasant level, enjoying (and suffering from) local self-sufficiency for most critical items of consumption. But in the Western world it is not so, and our enhanced vulnerability to any prolonged interruption of exchange patterns is correspondingly great. We have traded wealth and power for assured survival in time of disaster. It remains to be seen how the tradeoff will balance out across, say, a thousand years.

On the other hand, the regenerative capacity of modern industrial–commercial society is extraordinary. The recovery of Germany and Japan from World War II is a telling demonstration of what can be done when conditions are right. Yet their recoveries depended on transfusions from outside. If a truly global disaster should descend upon us, so that all existing high-technology societies suffered as much as several months' interruption of the exchange of goods and services that keep them alive, then regeneration would not be easy and might be impossible for centuries. Thus our enhanced powers are profoundly ambivalent as far as I can see. It has always been so, however. Every new skill brings new risks; and humanity has been accumulating skills and risks at an unprecedented pace lately.

Beyond Statistics

What the upshot may be, time alone will tell. Historians are only good for hindsight—and rather coarse-grained hindsight at that, especially when put into juxtaposition, as in this panel discussion, with the modes of analysis to which economists are accustomed. Yet I believe historians' preoccupation with catastrophe might be useful to economists, if they care to listen. Extreme cases, breakdowns, abrupt interruptions of established market relations—these are not staples of economic theory, and are, I believe, usually dismissed by statistically minded analysts of the norm and its fluctuations. But human societies are a species of equilibrium, and equilibria are liable to catastrophe when, under special limiting conditions, small inputs may produce very large, often unforseen, and frequently irreversible outputs. I believe there is a branch of mathematics that deals with catastrophe—sudden changes in process; I must say that I, as an historian contemplating the richly catastrophic career of humanity across the centuries, venture to recommend to economists a more attentive consideration of such models—at least when trying to contemplate the deeper past and long-range future.

Scientific Perspective
Lewis M. Branscomb
Vice President and Chief Scientist, IBM Corporation

My message is a simple one: technology can give us plenty of alternatives. But coping with an uncertain future requires a healthy respect for the unpredictability of nature and the limitations of our knowledge. Our problem is not fear of technology, but an unwillingness to face up to the responsibilities that go with its opportunities.

People today are dismayed at forecasts of a bleak future of exhausted resources and social turmoil on a polluted, overpopulated planet. Yet, the technophobes are outnumbered by those who ask too much from science and technology. We are told that we have a right to expect a better future than previous generations ever thought was possible, let alone was their right to demand. However you may choose to measure the quality of life, or weigh the maldistribution of the most valued benefits—there has certainly been a revolution of expectations.

Indeed, from a global point of view, the revolution in expectations for more widely shared access to the fruits of technology is fueled by falling death rates, increased urbanization, and the accessibility of global communications. Political turbulence in the Third World is a reflection of these expectations. At home the scientific community shudders at the phrase "war on cancer," implying that the expenditure of public money is the only substantial obstacle to the elimination of this disease. We are told that there is enough coal and fissionable material to last us many decades. When these run out, technologies for solar, fusion, and biological fuel systems can be invoked. It is just a matter of time and permissive cost. Why, then, do we seem to be losing the first battle in what President Carter calls the "moral equivalent of war"? The so-called energy crisis and, indeed, most of the other crises that are overloading the consensus-making institutions in our democracy, are crises of confidence and will. These crises result when the positive potential of technological alternatives encounters the limitations of both centralized (public policy) and decentralized (competitive market) mechanisms for decision making.

Obviously, we—collectively—are not managing our affairs well. Maybe we never did, but now the circumstances are different. Today there is something we can do about many of our problems. That something derives from the potential of new technology. Thus, I contend that while future shock from coping with the social consequences of technological change does make it harder for a lot of people to cope, the real problem is coping with the gap between what is and what could be.

The problems are thus primarily political, social, and economic. But if the stress that results from coping in these spheres proves too traumatic, the result may be to suppress the very resources of science and technology that give rise to the new expectations in the first place.

Overburdening the Courts

The case that a democracy may be fatally stressed by conflicting values and expectations born of new possibilities deserves a careful hearing. Our government was designed deliberately to make decisions difficult. Divided authority and protection of minority views are our first defense against tyranny. Conducting the government's business is a complex process of consensus building. It is no wonder that most of our senators, congressmen and executives in government are lawyers. They are trained to master complex facts quickly, if superficially, and to search for the common denominator of action that will resolve conflicts. Where conflicting views cannot be accommodated, the problem is somehow ducked or postponed. Reducing or containing conflict is, after all, the first priority in a democracy. Planning for an uncertain future must come second.

I believe that this explains why such a large burden for resolving scientific and technological issues in public policy has been thrown on the courts. The National Environmental Protection Act (NEPA) is, in my view, the most significant and far-reaching legislative innovation of the past quarter-century. It has made the courts a primary instrument for balancing incommensurate values—weighing the survival of the Furbish Lousewort against economic development in Maine, to assessing the need for fuel in central states against the fear of pollution in our coastal ports and shores. Unhappily, the courts traditionally look backward to precedent and to established fact; they are ill-equipped to look into the future in order to deal with statistical uncertainty and damages or benefits yet to be realized. But even if our judges were equipped to generate the information required to guide today's actions in light of future consequences, I fear for the ultimate consequences to our most cherished political values. The judiciary can serve as a political safety valve only up to a point. Beyond that point the responsibility must come back to the people directly.

Thus, a well-informed electorate is the ultimate safeguard of our liberties, as indeed it has always been. But today, a substantial amount of scientific and technological literacy must be added to the growing burden of citizen responsibilities. What then should the citizen's view of the prospects for mankind be? We had better start with the myth of finite resources.

Lewis M. Branscomb

Finite Resources and Human Potential

To be sure, the material resources of the planet are finite, although in any practical sense the most abundant minerals in the earth's crust are effectively inexhaustible. There are specific materials that are—or could soon be in short supply—oil, chromium, and so forth. But we must remember that the reason they are in potentially short supply is a reflection of the particular mix of technologies that constitute our *de facto* technology strategy for materials. In fact, the spectrum of materials strategies made possible by science is so broad and is expanding so fast that it is very difficult to identify any function served by technology for which alternative materials solutions cannot be found.

The point is that the planet is *physically* finite. Its renewable, living resources are not only finite in amount, but may be irreversibly exhausted if their ecological balance is fatally upset. But the resource of physical and human resources, taken together, is open-ended as far as we know. In the language of the systems analyst, managing resources in the future is not a "zero sum game." Every action does not have to result in an eventual negative consequence of comparable magnitude. Energy can be traded off against not only materials, but even intangibles like information. Information is the ultimate renewable resource. Indeed, it improves and spreads in the very process of consumption. Thus the scope of choice open to mankind is determined not only by the material resources available today, but the hard and soft technologies that exist and can be generated for the future.

Even if convinced that our options are quite open-ended, it does not follow that coping with future uncertainty is made easier as a consequence. Indeed, the more options there are, the more uncertain is the course of future events. Choice is a precondition to coping; it is necessary but not sufficient. Private choice among many alternatives in a competitive enterprise environment will doubtless best satisfy the immediate needs and desires of the public. But the scale of human activity is such that private choice must operate within a context that is compatible with the future survival of human society under acceptable conditions. This context must account for the fact that human activity may transform the natural environment in irreversible ways. Changing fossil fuel to carbon dioxide may have climatological consequences of a seriously threatening character. By the time a statistically significant change in carbon dioxide concentration in the atmosphere is unambiguously established, it may be too late to avoid a deleterious effect on food production, for example. Of course, we do not know for certain that this would be the result of an energy strategy that emphasizes exploitation of coal reserves and effectively foregoes the nuclear option. And there are hazards associated with the nuclear alternative. But such issues must be faced, and decisions must be made before irreversible harms are suffered—even before science can prove to everyone's satisfaction that predictions of such effects can be relied on.

Zero Risk Versus Lost Opportunity

A second kind of long-term threat to our well-being must also be addressed. The highly complex arrangements that constitute the infrastructure of a modern industrial society are designed for efficiency, but not always for resiliency. Some hard lessons have been taught us by experience with electric power distribution. We have paid less attention than we should to the manner in which the man-made, as well as natural, environments respond to unlikely events. Arrangements that degrade slowly and are resilient to catastrophe are not necessarily hard to provide. They require flexibility, which can be obtained by technological options and appropriate institutional arrangements.

If, indeed, the issues we must face about the future involve substantial uncertainties and if we cannot identify where all the benefits and burdens may fall, how can sensible national and global strategies be generated? I have a few specific suggestions, which were contained in the report of the Bellagio Conference of the National Academy of Sciences in 1976.

Environmental impact statements and the notion of technology assessment, as currently practiced, seek to anticipate the consequences of human activity prior to the introduction of a technology about which we have little experience. Obviously, one should try to be as well informed as possible on the basis of projections, models, and theory. But we must find a way to permit the introduction of technological change in a prudent and graduated manner so that useful knowledge is gained early, and the technology can be evolved with the course of future events. Much recent legislation is written as though zero risk were a sensible goal. But the cost of lost opportunity carries its own risk. To learn what options are useful we must commit ourselves to quantify risks and benefits. That process itself cannot be without risk. We need more measurements and less guess work.

The second need is for improved public understanding. It is not sufficient for experts to advise the leadership. Unless the public understands the reasons for postponing early benefits for long-term safety or gain, the public simply will not allow the leadership—however well informed and enlightened—to make the hard decision. Thus public consensus—not political courage—stands between the scientists and engineers and their opportunity to contribute. When one considers the difficulty of arousing the public's attention and concern over matters of potential importance in the future, one can understand why most scientists fail in their attempts to communicate through the media. But the public measures scientific credibility by a standard unfamiliar to many scientists; that is, the ability to dramatize and simplify when communicating outside the group of recognized experts in one's field. This situation offers opportunities, but also temptations which can lead to corruption of the integrity of the scientific process.

The Financial and Institutional Challenge

Finally, early warning is not enough. We must develop institutions under a variety of sponsorships and arrangements to provide the facts and analysis required for anticipatory decisions. Such problem-oriented institutions should undertake substantive scientific, economic, and policy research and must be experienced and credible enough to deal with problems so riddled with uncertainties and hypothetical situations. Modeling the future as the basis for public decisions today is not a part-time or weekend task. There are few such institutions in the United States today; Resources for the Future is one of them. Why has the evident need not been filled?

The answer is that we have not developed a satisfactory way of financing this kind of research. The job to be done may be too big for private philanthropy alone, although some foundations have made an impressive start. Government appropriations are not the proper way to fund independent research that bears so directly on the balancing of values and interest, since government agencies, no less than private interests, have a way of knowing how the answers ought to come out. The Executive Branch agencies are parties at interest. The courts and the Congress need independent sources of analysis and expert testimony. To reduce the stress on the political process and to strengthen the public's ability to make informed choices, private initiative and support are essential.

Economic Perspective
Paul W. MacAvoy

Professor of Economics, Yale University

On the twenty-fifth anniversary of the founding of Resources for the Future, a great deal can be said about concern for the nation's resources that is not alarmist, overstated, or misplaced. The founding of RFF, following the Paley Commission's report, was called for on the premise that in a few decades the wolf would be at the door. On this anniversary, it is appropriate to indicate that the wolf is out there, but that he could well be held at bay for a while longer. The nation's resources, while more depleted and in shortage in some cases, have not been misused in ways that have reduced the capacity of the American economy, even though many of RFF's strictures and proposals for efficient use have been ignored.

Coping with the Gas Crisis

Certainly one of the most severe "shortages" in the nation's history, if not the worst, occurred in Ohio in January and February of 1976. Weather conditions across the nation were worse than in any winter in a hundred years, and natural gas deliveries were curtailed by the Columbia Gas

System to almost all factories, municipal buildings, and school systems in Ohio. The shortage was dealt with by substitution of other fuels, rearrangement of work schedules and school operations to times when fuels were not so necessary, and by simply reducing rates of consumption of energy of one kind or the other.

This shortage and its concomitant management by the company, state regulatory commissions, and the Federal Power Commission had been long foreseen by RFF's staff and other energy analysts in universities, corporations, and government agencies. Drastic policy measures had been proposed to prevent the shortage from occurring—such as the elimination of federal controls over prices and production of natural gas at the wellhead in the Southwest. But, rather than carry out such a measure, which the senators from Ohio regarded as a rip-off of Ohio citizens through producer price increases, the politics called for muddling through the winter with stopgap measures to manage the shortage. The results were to reduce employment and production by substantial amounts throughout the Ohio economy. But most of the losses, even in employment, were made up in the subsequent few months. The residual, in fact, mostly consisted of an outbreak of further state and national investigations of the competence of the Columbia

Gas System and of the allegation that producers were "withholding" gas during the freezing months of winter. Ultimately, additional legislation was enacted at the state level, calling for public divulgence of plans, prospects, and sources of supply of the Columbia Gas System. But there was, in fact, no sustained and disruptive shortage, and the immediate events had little effect on Ohio's economy in 1976.

Impact of Price Controls

The simple sequence of policy steps taken in recent years to manage natural gas crises follows the path leading to the very resource misuse or waste that was discussed in the Paley Commission's report. The exploration and development of gas supplies has proceeded from the most productive and advantageously located formations to those less well endowed, with the result that the marginal supply costs have been rising rapidly over time (possibly at the rate of 20 to 25 percent per annum). At the same time, the opportunity costs of the exploratory process have gradually shifted from gains foregone on shallow onshore drilling in such locations as the Panhandle of Texas to gains foregone on North Sea, West African, and Southeast Asian offshore drilling platforms (whose crude oil prices reach fifteen dollars or more per barrel).

Thus, while the costs of additional gas supplies have probably quadrupled in the last ten years, prices have not increased by anywhere near this magnitude, since they have been controlled by the FPC under court mandates since 1954. Price levels before 1970 barely exceeded $1.00 per barrel and annual increases did not keep up with the general rate of inflation. More recently, gas prices have approached levels one-half those of international crude oil, or roughly $8.50 per barrel crude oil equivalent. The price controls have bred profligacy in the use of natural gas on the part of industrial users of boiler fuel who have "grandfather" rights to supplies obtained in the 1950s. They also provided supplies to home consumers for heating at high temperatures, for extensive air conditioning, and for new uses such as ornamental lanterns, outdoor barbecue facilities, and saunas for customers connected to the so-called low-cost retail gas utilities. The only problem was the shortage creation inherent in the expanding demands. The depletion and profligate demands were met after 1970 by lessening supplies, until shortages developed to the extent of 20 percent of total demands.

It has taken almost twenty years for this misuse of scarce national resources to be made evident. The country has been left with a smaller stock of natural gas, while a wide variety of fore-

casters and prognosticators—including RFF—
were pointing out the likelihood that there were
more than sufficient, undiscovered and unde-
veloped reserves to replenish the stock, and perhaps even to hold it level for the rest of the
century.

It is likely that this type of regulatory policy
will be followed for other natural resources in the
next two decades. As new deposits become more
scarce and market prices rise, federal actions to
prevent further price increases will be taken to
avoid wealth or income losses on the part of
those consuming the original stock, whether they
be corporation or final consumer.

All of this will lead to excess demand, waste
in the use of resources, and short-term disruptions in the operations of the national economy.
Some of these effects may be marginally important. The natural gas shortage probably has, for
example, been important not because of last winter's rationing—the effects were transitory, as has
been argued—but because it has accounted for
most of the increase in imports of foreign crude
oil, which in turn accounts for the East Coast's
increasing vulnerability to embargo and disruption for short periods by OPEC nations. The
wastage of resources under price controls breeds
entrenchment and privilege, which has far-
reaching effects, including the wider application
of Nelson's Law (that is, the further away an

economy moves from market equilibrium, the less likely it will ever return because interest groups operating under the disequilibrium have much more to lose from such a return).

Coping with Another Embargo

Consider once again the probable impact of a significant embargo of the U.S. market by crude oil producers in the Middle East within the next few years. This would cause a significant diminution in supply, over a period ranging from one month up to one year, depending on how well the restriction and specification of purchaser would work over that period. This would cause a 10 percent reduction in total energy supplies, which—assuming fixed input–output relations—could in the extreme reduce the GNP by no more than half that percentage. But some part of that GNP would be much more valuable in final consumption than others, and those users with higher-valued output would bid away the remaining and more scarce supplies so that the price would increase and real GNP would decrease by far less than this percentage.

This is the likely sequence of events for a supply disruption in a natural resource over the coming decades. There are many ways in which it profits individuals and corporations to hold stocks against shortages or price increases, whether the commodities are coffee, energy resources, or bauxite deposits. Where the incentives to reduce risk of depletion are dampened by government controls—controls that prevent one from profiting from having held resources or materials—then there may be insufficient holdings. But these insufficiencies, as in natural gas, are not now nor can they ever be significant from the point of view of the economy as a whole. If they were to seriously threaten a recession, the governments themselves would either change the controls or begin holding stocks of resources (something governments seem attracted toward doing in any case).

Impact on Growth

Then, what is the concern with resource policies? The underlying issue is whether the path of GNP growth is steep or shallow—whether the rate of growth of the economy is kept somewhere near maximum level or allowed to be much less. The rate of growth depends upon investment in capital equipment, the rate of technical progress in capital and labor, and the level and growth of the labor force. That the wolf of depletion is at the door in natural gas, crude oil, and materials affects investment and technical progress. Investment is not for what would be more productive supplies of materials but rather is merely to replace aged and depleted stocks. More has been invested in projects to work around bottlenecks produced by the policy process in liquified natural gas, foreign natural gas pipelines, and non-OPEC foreign well drilling. This policy has induced the marginal productivity of energy investments and because of the importance of energy in the economy has thusly reduced the productivity of all investments.

To some extent, the new investment pattern has reduced the trend rate of growth of the American economy. What was a 4 percent growth path through most of the period since World War II has probably been reduced to a shallower path, somewhat closer to 3 percent per annum in the level of the real GNP. Some part of the reduction is due to reduced capital outlays, consequent upon the uncertainty and lower profitability of capacity in energy supplies and in raw materials generally. The contemporary consumers receive lower-priced (but higher-cost) supplies of resources at the expense of further generations who will find levels of the GNP lower after the turn of the century than they would have been if resources had been used more efficiently in more open markets in the 1970s. The wolf can explain this complicated matter to our grandchildren.

Environment and the Economy: Managing the Relationship

Charles L. Schultze

Chairman, Council of Economic Advisers

The theme I want to emphasize can be briefly stated: the achievement and the preservation of a reasonably clean and healthy environment imposes a set of requirements on the social institutions and the political skills of a free society that are both extremely demanding and significantly different from those that have served us well for other purposes in the past. I do not believe that we have yet developed the necessary institutions, or the necessary social skills; and as a consequence we are having now, and will continue to have, substantial difficulties in meeting our environmental goals while still preserving other economic and political values that we esteem very highly. Nor do I think that the solutions will become any easier as we move through the next twenty-five years toward RFF's Golden Jubilee.

When I talk about the environment, what I mean is not the environment in the narrow sense —not just clean air and water—but environmental esthetics, health and safety in the workplace, and the characteristics of the products we consume. More generally, I am talking about what we economists call the problem of externalities—that is, how to control the unwanted side effects of our production and consumption decisions. But I will concentrate on the problems of the environment as it is more narrowly described.

At the risk of some oversimplification, the role of the government in the United States— particularly the federal government—until recently was confined principally to a limited sphere of activities. These include producing or supporting the production of goods that private enterprise could not or should not handle; enforcing the rules of the game through contract law and antitrust policies; redressing through taxes and transfer payments the maldistribution of income; and for one reason or another, regulating a highly select sphere of private activities, such as transportation, electric utilities, and financial institutions.

But the chief characteristic of environmental and other health and safety side effects is that they are not restricted to any well-defined set of activities. Indeed, they are pervasive, running throughout the private production and consumption decisions of millions of business firms and hundreds of millions of consumers.

Ours is a highly affluent, urbanized, technologically advancing, economically dynamic, and chemically inventive society. And every one of these characteristics contributes to the magnitude and pervasiveness of environmental side effects. As we have grown more affluent, we have demanded more. When we earn our daily bread by the sweat of our brow, amenities are not very important. But environmental amenities become terribly important, the less we sweat and the more bread we have.

Urban conglomerations themselves tend to concentrate environmental damages and increase the likelihood of other side effects. Sheer physical closeness is an important cause of environmental problems. And because we are technologically advancing, we create not only new production techniques, but also new ways of despoiling the environment. And because we are a dynamic economy, firms and production processes are constantly shifting about, so that environmental standards in any one location—and in every location—have to change to accommodate the birth and death of firms and establishments. And finally, because we are chemically inventive, we are continually increasing the numbers of new chemical compounds whose yet unknown side effects may be dangerous.

The problem is not merely, or even principally, technological, nor is it even principally *economic* in the fundamental sense of the term. Devising technical solutions is not our problem. Our problems are really social and political. If there are limits to growth, the limits to growth are not going to arise from technological or resource factors. The limits to growth—and, in some very fundamental sense, the limits to choice as we try to handle these problems—are going to be determined by our ability to devise social institutions and to develop social skills capable of dealing with these kinds of pervasive problems.

How does society deal with such side effects, which are numerous, complex, pervasive, and acting on all our lives in different ways every day? How can we shape millions of individual decisions effectively toward social ends without strangling our other goals, especially economic growth and reasonable freedom of choice? How do we deal with millions of location decisions, changes in technologies and processes, and raw materials choices? What goods should be produced? What chemicals, fertilizers, and dyes should we allow or not allow, discourage or not discourage?

I do not pretend to have the answers to these questions, but I do want to suggest three directions in which we might move.

Commands or Incentives?

The first of these has to do with the way in which we as a society intervene in order to deal with environmental and other side effects. We usually tend to see but one way to solve such problems: we remove them from the decentralized, incentive-oriented market system and transfer them to a hierarchical command-and-control bureaucracy.

This seems such a clear-cut and simple way to do things. If you want to get something done —if you want, say, to reduce a polluting effluent —then specify the limits on that effluent for every firm that might put it into a river or into the air. Sometimes, specify the techniques of production. Sometimes, specify the raw materials to be used. Sometimes, specify what kind of treatment is to be given at the end of the pipe, or the chimney. In general, go at it in what appears to be a straightforward way; that is, determine what outcome is wanted, and by laws and regulations command that such an outcome be achieved.

And yet, this direct, hierarchical, command-and-control approach often is incapable of dealing with the complex problems we are trying to solve—precisely because we are dealing with such pervasive phenomena—millions of decisions under widely differing circumstances of costs and technology and raw materials, in widely differing regions, and reflecting widely differing tastes.

In a long series of studies, RFF has contrasted this command-and-control approach with an alternative form of social organization, one that attempts to use incentives and self-interest to achieve the common good. Essentially, what this second approach involves is recognizing that environmental damages are costs, and that in the normal course of economic life those who use scarce resources are required to pay the cost of those resources. It relies upon self-interest to achieve the kind of results we want. Elsewhere this approach has been elaborated at great length, and I am not going to repeat it here, but I do want to stress several points.

First, the incentive-based approach has limits. It is not a panacea. Although, on the whole, it does work, it cannot handle many kinds of problems. Where we are dealing not with questions of more or less, but of absolute zero, then the incentive system is unnecessarily complex. In such circumstances it is simpler to use regulations to ban or forbid. Some of the stickiest problems that must be faced in the future will be in the use of new chemicals and possible carcinogens. And here the fundamental problem, before we get to social institutions, is that we really do not understand their effects; we are faced with great uncertainty. And I, at least, do not know of any social system—large or small—that deals very well with problems of extremely large and highly uncertain damages. The kinds of decentralized, incentive-oriented institutions that might work well in many ways also are very difficult to apply here. But since that is also true of any system, I must—as the old Scots preacher said, coming to a difficult passage in the Bible—"look this difficulty firrrmly in the face and pass on."

Second, we are not starting from scratch in trying to introduce decentralized, incentive-oriented systems into handling the environment. We are starting with a complex of existing laws and regulations, and of interests, accomplishments, and failures, which are based pretty much on the hierarchical command-and-control technique. Even if we could reach an agreement, we cannot junk the existing system and substitute an alternative approach. Instead we have to find ways to make a gradual transition over the years from what we have now to what it is absolutely essential that we have in the years to come.

Finally, an incentive-oriented approach is really an attempt to create a new market for a set of valuable commodities that have not been treated in a market sense before: namely, the environment. And yet, we have not had, if you think of it, very much, if any, experience as a society in creating large new markets *de novo*. Most markets that we know about have emerged over time through years and decades—and, in some cases, generations—of trial and error; and the equilibrium that we now observe has resulted over time. How do we go about creating a large new market which—in terms that I described before—is very pervasive and complex?

With all these difficulties, I think we must rely on a different kind of social organization from the one we are now using to deal with the environment. We must do so for one critical reason: the future of our society is going to hinge, in part, on the discovery and adoption of ever-improving technologies in order to reduce the environmental consequences of expanding production. There is no way that we can achieve our purposes, nor in fact, continue to exist as an advancing society, without a continuing shift in the direction of technological change. And this is not a matter of a crash program—a Manhattan Project or a space project. We are dealing with a constant channeling and fostering of certain kinds of technologies relative to others. And it is here that the power of marketlike incentives and the forces of self-interest to stimulate and direct innovation is most critical. To put it another way, the static efficiency of marketlike approaches is small potatoes when compared with the long-term, dynamic efficiency.

Our living standards today are, by orders of magnitude, higher than those of the early seventeenth century. Had the triumph of the market meant merely that we used then-existing technologies more effectively, our increases in living standards would have been minuscule compared with what actually happened. And by analogy, if we look not just at the Golden Jubilee of RFF but at its centenary, then it is precisely that channeling of technology that is so critical. I am convinced that whatever regulation can do, it is extremely inept at pacing and channeling technology. It thus becomes necessary to harness the motivation and self-interest of individuals and firms to carry out this absolutely crucial task.

Setting Environmental Priorities

Let me turn to a second major area, of somewhat less importance, in which I think we can improve the capacity of our social institutions to deal with harmful environmental and other side effects. Over the years, we have developed an information planning and control mechanism through which the federal government, and other levels of government, can deal with the myriad activities that government carries on. We call that mechanism the budget.

Before the Budget and Accounting Act of 1921, individual departments and agencies of the federal government dealt with budget requests on their own, with no central direction. I am given to understand that there was a single clerk at the Treasury who would receive these departmental requests, bundle them up, and deliver them physically to the Congress. The Budget and Accounting Act brought that all together into a single— presumably, at least—presidentially controlled budget plan. This made it possible to look at the aggregate, and the relationships of the parts to the whole. This device has helped us to set priorities and to evaluate the economic impacts both of the aggregate and the pieces.

Nevertheless, it is imperfect. It is principally composed of costs, and, in most cases, we found no good way to measure benefits. But even with those drawbacks, it has become an obviously indispensable tool for setting priorities. Major improvements have been made in it over the years: The accounting techniques and systems have been improved; more informative and better categories have been devised; and all kinds of special analyses have been perfected so that we can look at the impacts of our programs in different cuts— for example, we can look at all the R&D programs together, all construction programs, or all grant-in-aid programs, and so forth.

In recent years, improvements in the congressional budget process have made it possible for the Congress to look at the budget as a whole, rather than piecemeal. And finally, we are beginning—imperfectly, fumblingly, with some hesitation—to introduce five-year budgets and longer-term planning into the budget exercise.

Now let us turn to regulatory activities—that is, regulations to control externalities and environmental activities. We find no analog to the setting of budgetary priorities. Most of the environmental costs are not budgetary costs or governmental costs. Instead they usually are incurred in the first instance by industry and then passed on in the price of the product. Nevertheless, they are real national costs; the resources used for this purpose cannot be utilized for other purposes. Both the benefits and the costs involved are very large. Depending upon how wide one casts one's net, and what particular estimates one uses, they already run into the scores of billions of dollars each year, and they are growing rapidly.

Thus it may be time to think about constructing a framework within which to plan and set priorities for environmental and related programs, analogous to the federal budget for direct-spending programs. The difficulties in doing this are, and would continue to be, formidable. Unlike most budgetary costs, the costs are incurred outside the federal government. It is sometimes very hard conceptually, let alone empirically, to measure cost. What do you do, for example, when an environmental regulation simply causes a shift from the use of one raw material to another? How do you measure the incremental cost? And if you can measure it in one year, what do you do over time once the switch has been made? There are widely varying estimates of the historical costs of our environmental programs, and even wider estimates of future costs. We know that costs in the regular federal budget are hard to project—you have heard of cost overruns—but they would be much harder to estimate here.

In addition to everything else, the normal federal budget is an instrument of explicit accounting control over costs, imposed explicitly on those who actually disburse the monies. And here again, the analogy with environmental costs falls down. Yet, the concept might be both feasible and useful as an informational device, as a planning tool, as an integrating device, and as a way to develop methods of setting priorities for what we want to accomplish and how rapidly it can be done. To a large extent our decisions now are taken piecemeal, not because of feuding agencies or an unwillingness to cooperate, but in many cases because we lack some action-forcing, integrating mechanism. And, imperfect as it is, the budget does force some such integration and cooperation.

Initially, the data for setting environmental priorities would be very rough and, if not used with great care, could be very misleading. The appropriate categories would have to be developed and would undoubtedly be gross at first.

Nevertheless, the attempt to construct such an instrument might itself produce better estimates and better data.

It is probably true that innovations like this are best developed initially outside government, or certainly outside as well as inside. Environmental control is and must remain a major national priority. Quite probably it does now and will continue to absorb increasing national resources of capital, labor, and materials. And over the years, it will also become increasingly necessary to develop an integrated informational and planning mechanism to guide policymakers in this area. The historical analogy of the budget is one device toward which we might look for such an integrating mechanism. At least, it might make an item for a research agenda both within and outside the government.

Price and Wage Escalation

Let me turn now to the third point I wanted to make, one that is also of a somewhat lower order of priority. It involves the way in which the costs of environmental improvement enter into the wage- and price-setting mechanism. Although a shorter-run problem, it nevertheless is a significant one.

Improving the environment in the broader sense of the term is costly, drawing on resources that could have been used elsewhere. The costs must be paid. But the gains, in the form of environmental improvements, are not captured in our national income and other accounting data generally. Better access to cleaner air, for example, does not show up as an increase in the GNP. What we do when we make environmental improvements is to accept lower economic growth, as conventionally measured, in return for an increment in unmeasured output, or welfare. And if we choose wisely, the national welfare is improved, even if the measured growth in national income is reduced.

Necessarily, we have imperfect measures of national well-being, but since we are aware of this limitation, let us set aside the question of how we determine whether we are better off and turn to a related question, How this process of accepting lower measured growth for increases in welfare intrudes on the setting of wages and prices?

Environmental improvements lead to higher costs of production in the steel industry, the paper industry, or the aluminum industry. They may also increase transportation costs in these industries by shifting plants to less efficient locations. As a consequence, prices of these products rise. We pay a higher price for steel because, in addition to the steel, we are getting some increment in the environmental condition. Higher prices for these products, and for goods that are made from them, will slow down the growth in real wages as they are conventionally measured. That is, precisely because our price indexes reflect environmental costs as well as other costs, the process of improving the environment necessarily means— everything else being equal—that when changes in wages are divided by changes in the consumer price index, the measure of real growth will be lower than it otherwise would be. And this is simply a reflection of the fact that we are giving up some real income—as conventionally measured—for something else.

Over the years we have tried to insulate ourselves from changes in the cost of living. Formal escalators in many wage contracts provide that wages will be raised automatically to compensate for price increases. Other contracts and government programs also escalate various costs, benefits, or remuneration by changes in the measured price indexes. We have developed a partial mechanism for trying to escape the reductions in measured real income growth resulting from price increases, such as those that environmental improvements impose.

As a result of these escalations, environmental improvements impose an additional source of inflationary pressure, not simply in the first round of the price increase, but in subsequent rounds, when the rise in the price index automatically leads to increases in wages and other prices. This increase is not huge. It is not going to bring society to a screeching halt, but it does add to the already difficult set of economic problems that we face. It increases the rigidities in our wage–price mechanism, and makes it more difficult to bring inflation under control during a period in which we are trying to make significant environmental improvements.

I am not suggesting that we change the consumer price index; it measures what it is supposed to measure. It measures the price of steel. If raw material costs go up in steel, we include that rise as an increase in the price; and if environmental improvements—which are a cost—go up, we ought to let it show up in the price of steel. But it might be useful to develop—at least as an educational device—measures of changes in prices and real incomes that exclude the effects of environmental costs.

Again, we face major difficulties. We would have to approximate data, and analytical concepts; but I suggest it might be very useful to develop such indexes in order to indicate what kind of real cost increases are inescapable. Perhaps with a better understanding of the cost of achieving our environmental objectives, we can explore ways to reduce their second- and third-round inflationary impacts.

Appendix

Program for the Forum marking the 25th anniversary of the founding of Resources for the Future, held on October 13, 1977, in Washington, D.C.

Forum Program

Morning Session

Alexander Heard, Chairman of the Board,
Ford Foundation
Chancellor, Vanderbilt University, presiding

Introduction to the Conference
Charles J. Hitch, President,
Resources for the Future

Resources in the Past and for the Future
Edward S. Mason, Dean Emeritus,
Harvard University
Honorary Member, Board of Directors,
Resources for the Future

Emerging Global Resource and Environmental Problems
Harrison Brown, Director
Resource Systems Institute, East-West Center
Member, Board of Directors,
Resources for the Future

Luncheon

Alice M. Rivlin, Director,
Congressional Budget Office, presiding

Energy Imperatives and the Environment
Robert W. Fri, former Deputy Administrator of
the Environmental Protection Agency and the
Energy Research and Development
Administration

Afternoon Session

Joseph L. Fisher, Member of Congress
and former President of Resources for the Future,
presiding

Coping with an Uncertain Future
Historical, Scientific, and Economic Perspectives
William H. McNeill, Professor of History,
University of Chicago
Lewis M. Branscomb, Vice President and Chief
Scientist, IBM Corporation
Paul W. MacAvoy, Professor of Economics,
Yale University and former Member, Council of
Economic Advisers

Evening Program

Charles J. Hitch, presiding

Reflections on This Day
Gilbert F. White, Professor of Geography,
University of Colorado, Chairman of the Board,
Resources for the Future

Introduction of Speaker
William S. Paley, Chairman of the Board,
CBS, Inc., and former Chairman of the Board,
Resources for the Future

The Environment and the Economy: Managing the Relationship
Charles L. Schultze, Chairman,
Council of Economic Advisers